10/23/21

BASEBALL'S  FUTURE

ANALYTICS AND BEYOND

ANALYSIS BY FORMER PROFESSIONAL BASEBALL PLAYER

BILL DAVIDSON

Bill Davidson

Wasteland Press
www.wastelandpress.net
Shelbyville, KY USA

Baseball's Future:
Analytics and Beyond
by Bill Davidson

First Printing – March 2021
Paperback ISBN: 978-1-68111-396-8
Hardback ISBN: 978-1-68111-397-5
Library of Congress Control Number: 2021904249

Printed in the U.S.A.

0 1 2 3 4

To my wife, Ellen:

Encouragement personified

ACKNOWLEDGEMENTS

Family members play an important role in our lives. My wife Ellen and I just celebrated our eighteenth anniversary. As with my first book: *Dugouts, Icons And Dreams*, Ellen, a former English, French, and Spanish teacher, has given her full support in my current book writing endeavor. My parents are deceased. I have two sons from a previous marriage. Will lives in Asheville, North Carolina, and is engaged to April Spencer. Ben lives in Denver, Colorado, with his wife Karen, daughter Kyla, and son Evan. We try to visit as often as possible. I have three sisters: Jane lives in Delran, New Jersey, with her husband Jim O'Donnell; Trudy lives in Palmyra, New Jersey, with her husband Jim Ackley; and Kathy also lives in Palmyra, New Jersey.

Ellen has two daughters and a son from a previous marriage. Her daughter Kim lives in Lumberton, New Jersey, with her husband Paul Nave and two sons – Paul and Alex. Her daughter Niki lives in Cherry Hill, New Jersey, with her husband Wilson Mercado. Her son Ted Page lives in Wyomissing, Pennsylvania. Living near each other, we interact frequently.

Special thanks go out to Richard Pisani for helping with his computer expertise. Richard also helped with my first book.

Special thanks also to B. J. Ward for taking the time to edit my *Analytics in Baseball* poem in the beginning of the book. B.J. is a well-known, award-winning poet from New Jersey. I've attended several of his readings, and it was an honor to have him critique my poem.

My Chapter 17: Interviews exceeded my expectations of including it in my book. Thank you to all of those who participated. I won't list all of the names here; however, they are recognized along with their opinions in that chapter.

I want to acknowledge a list of friends who wished me good luck on my book. A special group of close friends: Ron Rossi, Bob Nutt, Gino Massimi, Bob Ward, and Bob Gini.

Another luncheon group, led by the legendary Al Harris: Al Morton, Jerry Campbell, Rocky Iacovone, Billy Kneller, Harold "Fudgy" Brooks, Butch Valeriano, and Bob Vanetten.

My Thursday golf group: Andy Taormina, Ed Shivers, Richard "Whip" Wilson, his uncle Richard "Duke" Wilson, Franny James, Greg Masters, Frank Hicks, Jerry Giser, Neal Kline, Ted Jamison, Jimmy Martin, Jim Kelly, Tom Brabson, Tom McKeown, Tony Fazzi, Dan Bobo, and of course Golden Pheasant Golf Pro, Brian Feldschneider. I thank all of you for your interest.

Others who expressed interest: Sharon McDermott, Bill Kurdyla, Ron Kashon, Tom Feltenberger, Bill Strauss, Gary Morrison, Jay and Karen Phillips, Bill Holscher, and Vince and Marie Jennings.

Finally, I am confident that my editor Susan Giffin and publisher Tim Renfrow will provide the same professional touch to this book as they did in my first.

On Analytics and Baseball

by Bill Davidson

Baseball purists and fans are hoping to stave
traditional elements from dying.
Yogi and Casey each stirring in his grave.
Are analytics and progress dying?

Could Pete Rose – the "Hit King" – teach hitting today?
No, when questioned in an interview.
"Launching" would not be his method or way
to succeed, requiring further review.

"Where have you gone, Joe DiMaggio?"
was a famous line in *The Graduate*.
Similar thoughts could be imagined
in determining if analytics is adequate.

Infielders influenced by analytic "shifting"
create an acrobatic double play attempt.
Fans' memories are left lamenting
where the "good old days" went.

Not to be outdone, the outfielders shift
to pastures previously unknown,
leaving behind vast empty "gifts"
for hitters to expose the known.

Hitters no longer strive to advance
runners on second with zero outs to third.
Time-tested strategy designed to enhance
a team's chance to win, no longer observed.

Having enjoyed an eleven-year professional
baseball career and even written a book
qualifies me to be somewhat critical
and cause the "experts" to have a second look.

Inspired by my baseball instincts
and analytics permeating the sport,
I have concerns for the game's extinction.
Hopefully, tradition is a saving retort.

CONTENTS

PROLOGUE

I would like to establish one thing at the outset. This is not an anti-analytics book. My fervent goal is to make "analytic" baseball understandable to the *average* baseball fan. I believe this is not happening today. We have been deluged with theories involving analytics. Launching, shifting, and exit-speed, to name a few. Owners, general managers – many of them Ivy League graduates – have invaded professional baseball with their textbook ideas, *selling* them to teams, despite any empirical evidence of long-term success. Books like *Money Ball*, *Power Ball*, *The MVP Machine,* and others have served to support their theories.

Fans are crying, "Who cares?" Each year, only one team survives and not necessarily the most analytical. How about good pitching, sound fundamentals, and use of time-honored theories? Instead of belittling these theories as "small ball", statistics should be produced to prove that not paying attention to small details can lead to losses. One or two losses can cost a playoff spot or an eventual chance to compete in the World Series.

After exhaustive research, including books, interviews, and various compilations of baseball analytics, I have drawn a few conclusions. Pitching and hitting must be stressed, with pitching correctly given number one status. Pitching is certainly the "name of the game." However, defense is given a low priority, with the exception of "shifting." Defense is given little attention. It is often relegated to an insignificant role, placing it in a traditional "small ball" context. I'll dispute this in various chapters. The authors present their Analytical Era case by demeaning the Traditional Era methods. Increased data is great, however, I make no apologies for having played in an era – the 1950s and 60s, when the best baseball was played, and the best players performed for the fans. An era when MLB had only eight teams in each league. Competition was keen, causing a backlog at the Minor League level. AA and AAA teams were loaded with players waiting for an opportunity. AAA had *three* leagues – American Association, International League, and the Pacific Coast League. Today's "watered down" version – thirty teams – provides more opportunities for players that would have had a tough time making it in AAA in those days. I'm talking about bench players and even some regulars, not the star players.

I suppose the "poster boy" for the Analytical Era would be Jose Altuve, the talented second baseman for the Houston Astros. He is a great player and due to his short stature, 5'5, an exception. He hits for average and power. If you're an Astro fan, you love him. More people would love him, if not for his "hot dog" style. He will hop over the dugout railing and chest bump his teammates for the benefit of TV. Same act after hitting a home run. Someone forgot to tell him to "act like he has been there before." I'll take Mickey Mantle's simple trot around the bases after a home run. Just my opinion!

I will deal with these theories in separate chapters. The average fan wants to enjoy the game. Baseball nuances will further your knowledge and enjoyment. Definitions will serve as a guide while reading the book and watching games during the season.

I just witnessed the demise of the 2019 Philadelphia Phillies. A top-heavy analytics management team wasn't the only reason for failure; however, it was a classic example of stubborn leadership overdoing analytics. My neighbor, Ken Ford, a longtime Phillies fan, aptly expressed his opinion in one word: Micromanagement.

Play ball!

CHAPTER ONE
Context

> Making the simple complicated is commonplace; making the complicated simple, awesomely simple. That's creativity.
>
> - Charles Mingus

Context defined: the parts of a written or spoken statement that precede or follow a specific word or passage, usually influencing its meaning or effect.

As I'm writing this, it occurred to me that this could be one of the most important chapters of this book on analytics, in keeping with my goal to write so that the *average* baseball fan can understand. To accomplish this goal, context becomes very important. Tune into any Major League Baseball game, and you are bombarded with statements from the announcers, usually a play-by-play announcer and a color commentator. The color commentator generally adds his *expertise* on a particular play.

The 2019 World Series between the Houston Astros and the Washington Nationals featured play-by-play announcer Joe Buck and color commentator John Smoltz. These two men treated fans to a non-stop dialogue on every play. I turned the sound off for the first time in memory. Terms like launch angle, spin rate, and exit speed were routinely tossed around. These terms could have been used as "teachable moments," adding meaning to the dialogue. Context.

I suppose announcers don't have time to educate the fans, explaining what their meaningless declarations refer to, in other words, the context of the subject. Smoltz, a knowledgeable Hall of Fame pitcher, could provide such information. That would be better than his endless, air-filling gibberish. Smoltz and Buck obviously don't believe in an occasional moment of silence. Perhaps Major League Baseball has a responsibility to usher in this analytical era with more *context* information? In the absence of this, I'll try to keep my promise and fill in the blanks.

In my chapter on definitions, I list analytic terms and their context. I also cite examples to serve as a *guide* for the average fan. While this is a short chapter, it is long in importance.

CHAPTER TWO

Pre-Analytical Era

Then: 1956 – Now: 2020

> We live in the present, we dream of the future, but
> we learn eternal truths from the past.
> - Madame Chiang Kai-Shek

Where do I begin? I was listening to some music and a golden oldie was playing. The late Andy Williams was singing his adaptation of "Love Story,"[1] a musical written by Stephen Clark, inspired by Erich Segal's best-selling novel by the same name. I love his lyrics, starting with "Where do I begin?" As a music lover (with great diversity, from Frank Sinatra to Pink Floyd and country music in between), I find it incredible that music can provide so much inspiration. In my first book, the Grand Ole Opry and Neil Young reflections got me started.

---

[1] Andy Williams, "Love Story," Musical: Stephen Clark, Novel: Erich Segal, wikipedia>wiki>Love_Story<A...

As I begin, I find it necessary to establish a few facts. I frequently hear how today's players are bigger, stronger, and faster than yesteryear's players which doesn't equate to better. I rarely read or hear any mention of some big, important differences. In the 60s, there were 16 teams, 8 in each league (American and National). Today, there are 30 teams, 15 in each league. Obviously, baseball is "watered down." Result: more opportunities for players. AAA in the Yankee organization in the 60s would be like the Majors today. There are average players in MLB that would have had a hard time making our AAA team. Of course, I'm not talking about the star players. Thirty vs. sixteen is a huge difference. This trickled down to the high minors AA and AAA, causing a logjam of talent. These players today have more opportunities. As I'll repeat, I haven't heard this conversation in my research. Too much time is spent praising today's players and their analytic-backed value and downplaying the past players and small ball traditional values.

Year: 1959

League: International AAA

Manager: Pepper Martin

Team: Miami Marlins

Subject: Clubhouse meeting

This is a scene that took place on every team I played for during my eleven-year Professional Baseball career. Each "new" three- or four-game series was preceded by a meeting, usually after batting practice the first night. We discussed opposition hitters' and pitchers' weaknesses and tendencies. This was our analytics. No super McCray computer. However, we utilized player and manager input. We set up our defense accordingly, shifting and so on but not to today's extreme. As I state in other chapters, too extreme can be troublesome. In retrospect, would we have liked more data? Sure, but certainly not at the expense of the traditional methods we valued. Pepper Martin was an unforgettable character, about whom I wrote in my first book. He held a clubhouse meeting every night. He was serious, but his humorous personality kept everyone loose.

Year: 1960

League: American Association AAA

Manager: Enos Slaughter

Team: Houston Buffs

Subject: Clubhouse meeting

Once again, our analytics were put to a test. We survived without computers; however, our traditional methods remained intact. I cover these methods – shifting, keeping the double play in order, etc., throughout this book. I recall a humorous incident at one of our meetings. Someone mentioned a player that I had played against earlier in my career. He had a slight build, and I offered the comment that he had concealed power. Laughter followed. Data accepted.

My purpose in citing these examples is twofold: (1) to show that data was important in the past, and (2) to show the differences in usage of the data. It would be an understatement to say that today's data far exceeds the past. Yet, analytics proponents' use of the data leaves a lot to be desired. Readers need only to refer to Chapter 13 on the double play to see a prime example. Fans deserve better. School is still out on the overuse of analytics, and MLB should take notice.

A good friend of mine – Ron Rossi – was an outstanding high school athlete. We were obviously among the top athletes in our era, mid-1950s and 60s. Ron signed with the Dodgers and I with the Yankees. These were the top two fundamentally sound organizations in baseball. I tell this story because it ties in with the overall analytical theories. One year, I had a short day in spring training in Florida and decided to visit Ron at his camp. I was training in Fort Lauderdale, and Ron was at Vero Beach. The contrast between the two camps was overwhelming. Ron was *imprisoned* in "Dodgertown,"[2] a facility conceived by President and General Manager Branch Rickey[3] in the late 1940s. It was a huge

---

[2] Dodgertown, www.baseball_reference.com/bullpen/Branch_Rickey.

[3] Ibid.

former naval base. Rickey was "analytically" ahead of his time. This complex provided spring training for all players from Class D to the Major Leagues. He wanted each player to be trained the "Dodger" way! Rickey, a former University of Michigan head baseball coach for four years, was also an inventor. He invented the batting helmet and the sliding pit, and he designed the batting cage. Ron was in good hands! Remember, I had just departed my spring training base in Fort Lauderdale which had a country club atmosphere, ONE team – AAA Richmond. It was a stark contrast. Dodgertown reminded me of my Marine Corps boot camp assignment at the notorious Paris Island in South Carolina, a Marine Corps base. It was good to *visit* Ron.

This story reminds me of the current happenings in baseball. The Houston Astros, a great team, is doing away with their bottom-level farm teams. It is part of a general MLB idea for "contraction", in Minor League ball. Teams – Houston in particular – want their entry-level players to be instructed in their "analytical" labs or spring training complex. Edgerton cameras,[4] weighted baseballs, GPS trackers attached to players backs, wearing sensors, etc., would hopefully give the Astros an edge. In a later chapter, I'll discuss this contraction in more detail.

Off-seasons today are spent, in many cases, in decrepit buildings with makeshift electronic devices to record progress.

---

[4] Edgerton Cameras, Driveline Baseball.com/product-category

These people would laugh at the off-season routines that Ron and I executed. We would often go to the gym in Bishop Eustace Preparatory School in Cherry Hill, New Jersey, and scrimmage with the high school basketball team as we both had played basketball in high school (no specialization like today's players). Or we would have a catch and do some running. We were getting ready for spring training. No cameras, no computers, no data. I'm glad we played in our "Golden Era" that arguably was equal to any, all things considered. Just my opinion!

CHAPTER THREE

Analytical Era / Present to ?

Have no fear of change as such and on the other hand, no liking for it merely for its own sake.
- Robert Moses

When I initially decided to write a book on analytics, I knew it would require an enormous amount of research. However, considering its presentation, it didn't reflect my viewpoints from a former player's perspective. I had a lot to say and knew I was up against the modern analytical era of baseball. Little did I know that in real time, as I'm writing, MLB has big problems. Commissioner Rob Manfred has some big decisions to make. A sign-stealing scandal is the subject, with many underlying schemes attached to that subject. Analytics is in the forefront.

I left my chapter beginning intact which turns out to be rather prophetic. Returning to the current scandal, I'll outline the details. The Houston Astros got caught. The Astros used video feed from a centerfield camera to decode the catcher's signs. Players banged on trashcans in the dugout to alert batters about the incoming pitch. Sign stealing with the "naked eye" is legal and has been going on *forever.* When I played, we had expert "crooks." Some players, including myself, didn't want this information for fear of it being wrong. Pete Rose recently said he had declined the information. Look for an off-speed pitch, and you're liable to get hit in the head with a "surprise" fastball.

MLB Commissioner Manfred acted swiftly and suspended Houston Manager A.J. Hinch and General Manager Jeff Luhnow for the entire 2020 season. Houston received a fine of $5 million and some amateur draft picks. Houston, bending to pressure, fired Hinch and Luhnow. Days later, Boston Red Sox Manager Alex Cora and the Red Sox went under investigation. Cora was the 2017 bench coach for the Astros and developer of the sign-stealing system. Boston, reacting to bad public relations, fired Cora. Next: Carlos Beltran, the new manager for the New York Mets, lost his title before managing a single game. Beltran was a former Astros player, and the Mets didn't want the bad PR.

Things change. Houston's on top now and will have to deal with damage control. The "Poster Team" for analytics has lots of talent and should survive. As for fans, I'll cover this in a later chapter titled – FANS. I'm predicting Commissioner Manfred might crack down on analytical-driven camera usage in baseball. In my research, I'm reading about cameras all over the place: dugouts, bullpens, behind home plate, etc. Some of these temperamental, ultra-analytical-minded pitchers have even expressed anger at MLB cameras interfering with *their* Edgerton cameras, used to analyze their performance. I will cover this in detail in a later chapter on pitching.

This analytical movement is so comprehensive and evasive that I've decided to break it down into separate categories to accomplish my goal: making it understandable to the average fan. The interviews I conducted with fans (average and above average) confirmed my belief that without simplification, the subject becomes overwhelming. So far, the consensus appears to be that many fans are being turned off to the game, many to the point of no longer watching it. I hope that this book will at least alleviate some frustration for baseball fans.

CHAPTER FOUR
MLB / MONEY

> Baseball? It's just a game, as simple as a ball and a bat. Yet, as complex as the American Spirit it symbolizes. It's a sport, business, and sometimes even religion.
>
> - Ernie Harwell

It all starts at the top. MLB controls everything. If analytics were not accepted, it would be gone. They are all in. Fan attendance and TV ratings are being monitored. These ratings influence MLB decisions. Rule changes – some good, some bad, with the fan in mind – have had mixed results. Speeding up the game is a joke. Rules are in place for batters stepping out of the box after each pitch. They fix their batting gloves, socks, and whatever other body parts, and frequently call time out if they're not ready. The umpires are not enforcing the rules. Why? It's not that this is contributing significantly to the overall length of the game, but who wants to watch all of these rituals before every pitch? Many fans lament that this and other aspects of the game are making it too long. Studies have been made on just about every phase of the game – from increased commercials between innings, pitching changes, instant replays, and more.

Despite all of these annoyances, one MLB study showed that in 1984, games lasted 2.5 hours and in 2017, 3 hours.[1] These are average figures. I was surprised, as I'm sure most of you are as well. I guess it just seems like it's longer. I love the game, but I can read a book during most games.

I played against a player who would have fit right in with today's crop. His name was Lou Skizas. Casey Stengel called him the most *natural* right-handed hitter he ever saw. Lou played for the Havana Sugar Kings. I was with the Miami Marlins, managed by Pepper Martin, the most unforgettable character I ever met in my eleven-year career. It was in 1959 in the International League (AAA) with Fidel Castro in attendance. Lou would go through the usual routine prior to stepping into the batter's box: tugging his pants, fixing his socks, etc. Then he went through a ritual while the pitcher was getting his sign from the catcher. He would touch his hat, rub his nose, pull at his pants, all while the pitcher was winding up. But wait. The last thing he had to do was touch a rabbit's foot in his back pocket. It was unbelievable. Guys on the bench would bet on whether he would get his hands on the bat in time to hit. He always did, and most of the time, it was a line drive somewhere. The analytic launch angle advocates would have watched in awe.

---

[1] www.baseball-reference.com

I got a little sidetracked. Back to MLB calling all of the shots. These rule changes really affect the game. Pitching mounds have been raised and lowered at different times. Before 1968, the pitching mound height was 15 inches. It was called "Year of the Pitcher." They then lowered the mound to 10 inches. MLB felt baseball was becoming too pitcher friendly. Lowering the mound now favored the hitters.[2] From time immemorial, baseballs have been called juiced, especially after a big spike in home runs. Stitches can affect the ball. Here's the standard since 1934: 108 double stitches of waxed red thread (easier to see), cowhide leather, cork center, and all done by hand.[3] South Jersey tidbit: Mud from a secret spot in South Jersey off the Delaware River. The mud is called Lena Blackburne Original Baseball Rubbing Mud. Lena was a MLB player and coach with the Philadelphia Athletics. By the 1950s, the mud was used by all MLB teams.[4]

This past 2019 season, with an increase in home runs, has resurrected claims of the ball being juiced. Changing baseball specs can be very expensive. Close to 18 dozen balls per game equates to 300,000 per season, and 500,000 not used in games equals a million balls in one season. Figuring \$3.00 a ball to make all *exact* = \$\$\$. So change won't be made just to appease those that say the ball is more lively. Commissioner Rob Manfred says, "Same

---

[2] www.washingtonpost.com MLB after 1968s...

[3] https://www.quora.com>why-is-th...

[4] en.m.wikipedia.org

specs are used."[5] Lying? As the lyrics in a song ("Perfect Sense") by Roger Waters of Pink Floyd fame relates, "It all makes perfect sense, expressed in dollars and cents."[6]

As I'm writing this chapter, MLB has cancelled spring training (March 2020) due to the outbreak of coronavirus (COVID-19). Safety at this time is all important. Spring training has been suspended indefinitely. Regular season games might not occur until May or June. Players were told to go home. The start of spring training depends on the virus outlook. This certainly puts things in perspective. Players will have to get in baseball shape again. At first, players were going to stay only in Florida or Arizona. However, the emergency is projected to last a month or more. Now they're going home. Players from out of the U.S. are uncertain of their plans. Training might even resume in MLB cities, with exhibition games among teams in cities close to each other. Of course MLB problems are insignificant in view of the worldwide situation.

The last time baseball came to a halt was the infamous baseball strike in 1994-95. It was the eighth strike in baseball history, lasting 232 days (8/12/94 - 4/2/95). It proved to be the longest, covering the remainder of the season, postseason, and World Series. The normal number of games – 162 – became 113 in 1994 and 144 in 1995. The owners forced Commissioner Fay Vincent to resign. Bud Selig became the acting commissioner.

---

[5] www.Cleveland.com – Juiced balls?...

[6] Google Roger Waters Perfect Sense – STLyrics.com>R>Rogeer Waters

Play resumed again in the spring of 1995 under terms of the expired contract. Executive Director Donald Fehr didn't trust Selig. Spring training started with MLB using replacement players: Minor League players, retired Major League players, and others with zero professional baseball experience. This was all because of salary cap issues.[7] Money!

The strike was settled before the season opener by a New York District Court Judge (Sonia Sotomayor – now a Supreme Court Justice) with a court order.[8] Hard feelings were expressed throughout MLB. Scabs were spurned. Minor League players who had crossed the line and made it to the Majors later, paid the price. Some needed the money. Replacement players went home. They were mocked and sometimes referred to as truck drivers. It wasn't a pleasant period of baseball.

Back to the present. When MLB play does resume, all eyes will be on Houston. Opposing players have vocally condemned the Astro players, claiming games and perhaps championships were stolen from them. More than a few Astro players have been hit by pitches this spring, despite Commissioner Manfred's pre-spring warning against retaliation. Trevor Bauer mockingly alerted Astro hitters about the incoming pitch. Could be an interesting season for the Astros. The delay of the MLB season could be a blessing in disguise for Houston. The public's attention has been rightfully diverted.

---

[7] https://en.m.wikipedia.org – The 1994-95 MLB strike

[8] Ibid.

Pepper Martin

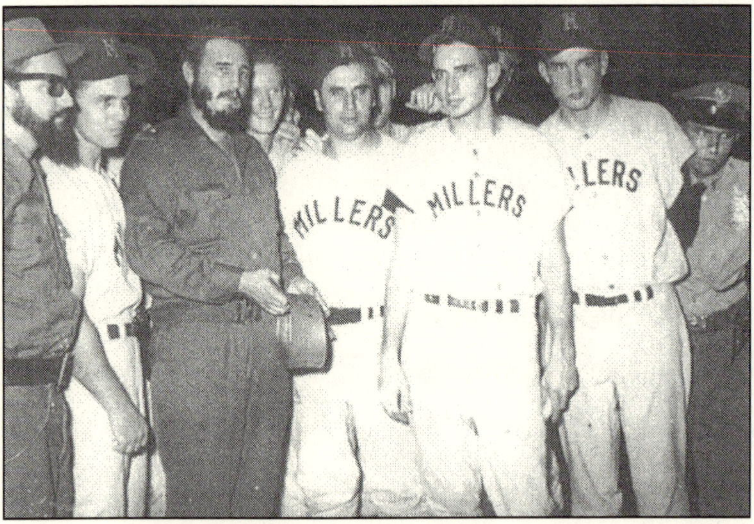

Fidel Castro - 1959
Manager Gene Mauch – second from left

CHAPTER FIVE

Pitching / Analytics

On Pitchers: "They cheat. They spit on the ball. They cut the ball. They're not a group with very good character. Never trust a pitcher. I wouldn't want my daughter to marry a pitcher."
- Richie Ashburn

I have to agree with Richie Ashburn's assessment of pitchers, although I won't be as harsh. Pitchers are a different breed. Past perceptions actually labeled them as non-athletes. The thought was that they did very little running and fielding and weren't expected to hit. Of course there were exceptions. Today's pitchers are generally bigger and perhaps stronger. Training methods have improved and analytic proponents will say they are better. They still can't hit, run or field, again with some exceptions. They pitch every fourth or fifth day, giving them plenty of "thinking" time in between. They are perfect candidates for today's analytics-driven game, with plenty of time for thinking and tinkering with their pitching theories. Pitching is the name of the game, and this group is in charge. Fans rooting for their favorite team can forget about their chances, without good starters and relievers, regardless of the starting lineup. Mike Trout and the Los Angeles Angels are a case in point.

As a shortstop for eleven professional baseball seasons, I've had my share of pitching experiences and education. Both teammates and opposition have provided this opportunity. Some pitching teammates: Phil Niekro, Mike Marshall, Barney Shultz, Al Lary, Al Schroll, Harry Perkowski, Mickey McDermott, Dave DeBusschere (yes, the great NY Knicks Basketball Hall of Famer), Fred Talbot, John Hiller, and Pat Dobson, to name a few. Some opposing pitchers: Bob Gibson, Denny McClain, Jim O'Toole, Ted Abernathy, Phil Niekro, Juan Pizarro, Jackie Collum, Jim Golden, Art Fowler, Ron Perranoski, Don Larsen, and Hoyt Wilhelm, to name a few.

Let me digress a bit before I journey into analytics. I have to start with my former teammate and roommate, Mike Marshall. This was in the 1960s in Montgomery, Alabama. It was toward the end of my career with the Detroit Tigers organization. Mike was somewhat of a *character.* I was probably one of the few guys on our team who got along with him. He cared not at all with his eccentricities and huge ego. We roomed together on road trips. We even played golf occasionally.

One game, after giving up a run and *stewing* in the dugout, Mike shouted to me, "You should have had that ball" on a base hit in the shortstop hole.

I yelled back, "Are you kidding me? That was like a shot out of a cannon." He was just that way.

I laughed at most of his antics. His wife, sitting in the stands with the other wives, would shout, "Come on, Mike, do it by yourself."

In sports, there's an unwritten rule: Never blame your teammates. Mike was friends with Jim Bouton, a Yankee pitcher who wrote *Ball Four*, a controversial book exposing teammates like Mickey Mantle and his carousing tendencies. Bobbie Bouton and Nancy Marshall, the players wives, consequently wrote a book in 1983 titled *Home Games*. This was after both had divorced their spouses and chronicled letters and journals in their controversial book. Very ironic.

Dave DeBusschere, the NBA Hall of Fame player, was also a good pitcher. Since basketball was my favorite sport, I was on a basketball scholarship at Temple University when the Yankee organization pirated me away. Dave and I had many spirited conversations. He told me the White Sox wanted him to give up basketball. He said, "I've got news for them, I'll probably give up baseball!" He did, eventually. He still spent a few years in the Major Leagues. I used to challenge him to one-on-one games on one condition, no "backing in" due to his 6'6" height. It never materialized, with the summer heat, etc. Just as well, reflecting on his NBA career.

Another teammate and roommate, pitcher Mickey McDermott, provided me with lifetime memories of his antics. This was while playing with the Miami Marlins in the AAA International League. Mickey was a nightclub singer in the off-season and good friends with Frank Sinatra. So many stories! He told me one story while he was playing with the Boston Red Sox. The Boston sportswriters were well known for their critical articles. Mickey, known for his free spirit personality, had a bad outing. The next day's headline began with *Juvenile Delinquent Mickey McDermott....* Dom DiMaggio said he would buy him a $200 suit if he punched the writer in the mouth. It never happened. He was too nice.

I'll tell one more story. Pepper Martin, our manager as I mentioned in Chapter 2, had a penchant for holding frequent clubhouse meetings. Well, Pepper would let the next night pitcher get his workout, shower. and watch the game from the stands. Mickey was scheduled to pitch the next night. At our usual meeting the next night, Pepper asked if he had seen a certain event. Mickey responded: "Hell, no, Pep. I was in a nightclub!" We all laughed, including Pepper.

I had the pleasure of playing with Phil Niekro and the displeasure of hitting against him. Knuckleball pitchers are hard to catch and hard to hit. The late Barney Shultz, my Houston teammate, had a good knuckleball. He became a pitching coach for the Cardinals and Cubs.

At the top of opposing pitchers I hit against is Hall of Famer Bob Gibson. He played for Omaha – AAA. I played for Denver. The year was 1959. I knew Bob threw hard. However, I was surprised to read he had reached 96.8 mph and even 107 mph during a demo. His fastball would rise in a hurry. What looked like a sure low pitch, about halfway to the plate, would end up a strike. It was hard to lay off a high pitch, causing many pop-ups. I doubt if launching techniques would have helped. Analytics advocates would counter that there are countless numbers of 95+ pitchers, both starters and relievers on MLB rosters. I find it hard to dispute that claim. However, how many of them have the necessary command of the velocity?

Denny McLain was the last MLB pitcher to win thirty games. Pitching for the Detroit Tigers in 1968, his record was 31-6.[1] I faced him in the minors. His fastball was similar to Bob Gibson.

I hit against Hoyt Wilhelm in a spring training game in Miami, Richmond vs. Baltimore Orioles. Brooks Robinson was playing third base. Good memories. After fouling off a few pitches, I drew a walk which I considered an accomplishment. Other knuckleball pitchers I played with or against, threw an occasional waste pitch (i.e., fastball). Not Hoyt, he threw a knuckleball every pitch. Incredible!

---

[1] Denny McLain, Pitcher, en.m.wikipedia

Jackie Collum was a good little left-handed pitcher. St. Paul (Dodgers) was in town for a four-game series in Denver. I remember hitting a home run off him, off the foul pole. Some of us stayed at a hotel in Denver, which had a restaurant and bar on the ground floor. After the game, we were having a beverage of our choice, and I spotted Jackie and some of his teammates. I sent him a beer. All in good fun! Unrelated to the pitching topic, this restaurant had great steak and eggs, perfect for a late breakfast after a late game, enabling us to get some extra sleep.

It's very difficult to compare pitchers or, for that matter, players from different eras. However, from this small sampling of outstanding pitchers, some in the Hall of Fame, as you can see the 50s and 60s weren't too shabby.

Most people, including myself, have either read the book *Moneyball* or have seen the movie. Even though the book could arguably be called the start of the analytical movement, it was dated material from 2003. I needed more updated information, and Amazon came to my rescue. I found many books on the subject. In retrospect, I made a good decision, purchasing two excellent books: *The MVP Machine*, written by Ben Lindbergh and Travis Sawchik, and *Power Ball*, written by Rob Neyer. These are very good, well-written books, and I would recommend them to any baseball fan. I don't necessarily agree with all of the contents, but they are informative. It also led me to research some of the topics on the internet to increase my knowledge. Purchase their books. You won't be disappointed.

In keeping with my goal to make this simple and understandable to the *average* fan, I may omit, in *some* cases, highly technical data, etc. If I do, I'll be certain to provide readers with information sources. These internet sources should satisfy any *advanced* students of the game

In the course of my extensive and comprehensive research journey, two names frequently surfaced. One a player and the other a sports complex. You might say the latter was ground zero for this analytical movement. The player: Trevor Bauer. The Sports Complex: Driveline. I'll provide details shortly. Of course, there are other players and facilities associated with analytics; however, this appears to be a starting point. Driveline Baseball is basically a sports facility founded by Kyle Boddy, a baseball trainer and consultant who stressed Sabermetrics, a method to improve performance.[2] I mention Trevor Bauer and Driveline for the simple reason that in my exhaustive research effort, it was very difficult to escape references to these two subjects. Other players have come on board in the advent of this analytical movement; however, Trevor is a unique individual. I'm very happy that I had Mike Marshall as a teammate and roommate, as their personalities are very similar.

---

[2] Driveline Baseball, Kyle Boddy, Trevor Bauer – Wikipedia.org

It helps me understand Bauer's idiosyncrasies and motivation. If you want to know more about Trevor Bauer, google the exhaustive number of books and articles that are available. I'll simply highlight some information to build my analytical point. High school seems to be a good starting point where Trevor was already showing signs of baseball interest and ability. His father naturally took notice and offered to help him by paying for lessons, and so on, provided he continued to work hard. No problem, Trevor was obsessed with baseball. A former college pitcher and friend of the family gave him private pitching lessons. Trevor's father, Warren, hired him.

Shortly after his lessons began, Trevor showed some improvement. He recommended that Trevor attend a baseball camp: Texas Baseball Ranch, located in Montgomery, Texas, 55 miles north of Houston.[3] This highly respected camp was loaded with instructors and training facilities and was a perfect fit for Trevor and his already sabermetric mindset. His father consented, and Trevor at age fourteen packed his bags. Therefore, Trevor, a nonconformist and nevertheless a hard worker, was ready for his high school baseball season. He did very well as a sophomore and junior on the field.

Off the field, his attitude was a precursor for his college and professional careers. In high school, his ideas and the coaches'

---

[3] Texas Baseball Ranch, https://vault.si.com/vault/2011/08/15/Trevor Bauer-bauer-will-not-be-babied/Lee Jenkins.

clashed. He ended up quitting the high school team in his senior year. The following year, he went to UCLA, exhibiting the same attitude and problems. You guessed it. The same problems prevailed in his professional career.[4] You may wonder why I spend so much time on this player; however, he is such a key figure in this analytical movement, it is unavoidable. Trevor exhibited obsessive, arrogant, and nonconformist qualities that would characterize his actions throughout his career.

Despite his abrasive personality, like Mike Marshall with his PhD in Kinesiology, you have to respect Trevor's intelligence and knowledge of biomechanics in baseball. So Trevor enrolled in UCLA, performed well, and continued his off-field personality shortcomings. He wasn't about to change. The 2011 MLB draft was coming up soon. The team's best pitcher Gerrit Cole and Trevor were two of the best players in the draft. Trevor was selected #3 by the Arizona Diamondbacks. The fit was disastrous. Teammates and coaches clashed over Trevor's attitude. (That reminds me of Marshall.) He was traded to Cleveland.[5]

As I mentioned earlier, along with Trevor Bauer, another name emerged frequently while researching analytics: Driveline Baseball. First, a little background on Driveline. In 2008 Kyle Boddy started a blog called Driveline. He had read an article by my old roommate, Mike Marshall (now Dr. Mike), on a theory called

---

[4] Ibid.Trevor Bauer, High School, College

[5] Ibid, Trevor Bauer, Professional

driveline. Mike used plastic javelins to promote a straight driveline toward the target. The driveline was one of Mike's favorite concepts. Boddy borrowed the name for his blog and later on for his business: Driveline Baseball.[6] He built a makeshift lab – batting cage, weights, etc., to teach his Sabermetric theories. In 2012 he moved to a larger location, nothing fancy, just more equipment.

So getting back to Trevor, in 2014 while working out in the off-season at Texas Baseball Ranch, Kyle Boddy was a guest speaker, and Trevor was enthralled. The two became friends. Although Trevor had spent his younger years at Texas Baseball Ranch, it was at Driveline, a drab warehouse, located in Kent, Washington, a suburb of Seattle, that he honed his theories as a MLB player.[7] That warehouse became his analytics classroom.

---

[6] 247 sports mlb.Indians Article Boddy Bauer

[7] Ibid.

CHAPTER SIX
Pitching / Analytical Quest

Strive for excellence; you will get closer to perfection.
Strive for perfection; you will never be satisfied.
- Saul N. Miller, DDS

Now that we have a little background on some major players in this era of analytics and various testing grounds, let's examine some of the pitching principles they attempt to achieve. Please refer to the Definitions chapter for unfamiliar technical terms.

Velocity! Pitchers have always sought ways to increase speed or velocity, and this analytical era has sparked an all-out effort to achieve added speed in their pitching arsenal. One hundred miles per hour on the radar screen is the magic number. Meanwhile, modern technology has become available. Different eras have emerged. The PITCHf/x era probably started the data craze.[1] This

[1] PITCH/X Era.en.m.wikipedia.org

system measured release point, speed, movement, spin, and location, using two highly specialized cameras in MLB stadiums. MLB already had reports of a few teams (Astros?) investing in a Cray super computer, costing $500.000.[2] The PITCHf/x Era became the Statcast Era in 2015.[3] Increased data was ensured.

Is it any wonder that MLB has gone all-in on analytics? They have hired Statheads from top to bottom to support the movement. Owners striving to keep up with the competition are placing them in key positions such as general managers, coaches, etc. Players who filled these positions in the past better acquire analytical skills or they will be gone. I discuss this in a later Player Development chapter.

Let's start with a definition of a pitch. In technical terms, "a pitch is a combination of velocity, spin rate and spin axis."[4] The analytics poster boy, Trevor Bauer, is relentless in his ongoing quest to increase his spin rate by increasing his velocity. Bauer tested the use of pine tar and other substances and claims they have "significantly increased his spin rate. More spin = more swing and miss, as proven by Driveline!"[5]

Let's trudge onward. There are two types of spin – transverse and gyroscopic. Transverse = slider /curveball. Gyroscopic =

---

[2] Cray Computer.ftw.usatoday.com/2014/03

[3] Statcast Era. http://m.mlb.com/news/article/1119234412/statcast-primer-baseballwill...

[4] Trevor Bauer, *MVP book* – pitchdefinition, combination...p,110

[5] http://blogs.fangraphs.com/Trevor/bauer-might-have...

straight ball. Most pitchers spin the ball on a 6-degree downward plane. So most hitters swing up at the same angle. Pitchers are now trying for 8 degrees down on breaking balls and 4 degrees up on fastballs, "disguised so that hitters can't tell the difference."[6]

Brian Bannister, former MLB pitcher and Boston Red Sox VP of pitching and currently VP of Pitching Development for the San Francisco Giants, is an analytics wizard. He was a pitcher, but he also enjoys the analytic hitting vs. pitching process. Bannister thinks hitters are still "trying to hit the 8-degree down, with their 6-degree swing."[7] I suppose this has led to today's "pitching era," and hitters are trying to keep pace. If pitchers other than the Trevor Bauers of the world, i.e., deep-thinkers, ever master the spin principles, hitters will be hard pressed to combat the analytic advances.

Time out! Since pitching is probably the most important facet in baseball, we have to take a breather. Kinesiology majors need only apply. Analytics has turned pitching, a relatively simple skill, into a complex activity. While terms such as spin rate, spin axis, etc., are intellectually explainable, the practical applications are subject to evaluation. Topnotch pitchers have had some success through perseverance. These are mostly MLB players, who have the time and resources to grasp the theories involved. In my opinion, for the masses: for high school, college, minor leaguers, etc., it resembles a treatise on Einstein's theory of relativity.

---

[6] Ben Lindbergh/Travis Sawchik, The Mvp Machine, 326

[7] Ibid.

Training facilities are expensive. Injury risk is high, and application of learned analytic *theories is* difficult.

Keep in mind the Edgertronic cameras, Rapsodo radar and Statcast are available for analytical analysis. So, what you have here are pitchers watching videos of their performance, analyzing the data, and adjusting their thought processes accordingly. All of this in an effort to improve, which is what we all want to achieve. This works for some, for others not at all. In another chapter, hitters are doing likewise. It reminds me of golf. You tinker with your swing, searching for that comfort zone. Some guys analyze and improve, others don't. It's a constant battle. Yes, golf also has its analytics – videos, etc. If all the golf analytics worked for me, I would have been on the tour. Even heavy thinkers like Bauer and Marshall have their slumps. This holds true for both traditional and analytical era players.

Let's get back to velocity. I'll list a few of today's flame throwers.

Arnold Chapman (Yankees) 105.1 mph
Jordan Hicks (Cardinals) 104.2 mph
Mauricio Cabrera (Braves) 103.0 mph

Some old-timers:
Nolan Ryan (Astros) 108.5 mph Estimate: No Radar.
Steve Dalkowski (Orioles) 115.0 mph Estimate: No Radar[8]
(Minor Leagues)

---

[8] m.mlb.com>statcast>leaderboard>pitch speed.

Steve Dalkowski was a Baltimore Orioles minor leaguer whose pitch velocity made him somewhat of a folk figure. Steve played in the 1960s. I never had the opportunity to face him. My friend Ron Rossi said he faced him while playing in Macon, Georgia, a Dodger affiliate. I had heard of Steve's reputation. Ron said he ended up walking and states that Dalkowski was incredibly fast. Although radar guns weren't used at that time, many players placed his speed at 110 mph, maybe 115. Ron said he was very wild, adding up to a high discomfort level for hitters. Steve never made it to the Major Leagues; however, his legend lives on. Steve was a heavy drinker, continuing his alcoholism into retirement. He stopped drinking and received some monetary aid from the American Association of Professional Baseball Players. He resumed drinking and lost his financial aid. Suffering from dementia, he is currently living in a long-term health facility. Another example of alcoholism that plagued baseball players throughout its history.[9]

Since the subject is on pitchers and velocity, I must include a story from my time as a NY Yankee farmhand in the 1960s. From the time I signed with the Yankees, my contract was assigned to Richmond, Virginia (AAA). At that time, NY had two AAA teams, Richmond and Denver. One spring, they told Richmond to try out Fort Lauderdale, Florida, for the big club, deemed more than acceptable. The following year, the Yankees trained there, and

[9] wikipedia>wiki>Steve_Dalkowski

they shipped us to some obscure Florida town. I enjoyed Fort Lauderdale while it lasted.

So each spring, the Yankees would break camp and head north for the upcoming season. They traditionally stopped in Richmond for an exhibition game. We also broke camp and joined the Yankees on the northbound train. It was great – a parade to the ballpark, capacity crowd for the game, and a dinner that night featuring the malapropism of Casey Stengel and his Yogi Berra-like quotes.

On this team was a pitcher, Ryne Duren, whom I hoped I wouldn't have to face. I didn't. Phew! Bobby Shantz relieved that day, to my relief. Duren was a speed-baller who had very poor eyesight. His glasses were as thick as the bottom of a Coke bottle. He was a relief pitcher. While warming up, he would often throw at least one pitch over the catcher's head into the screen. Frank Crosetti told him to do it on purpose to intimidate the opposition. They didn't record speed back then; however, it surely was over 100 mph. Ryne unfortunately had an alcoholic problem for the duration of his career. He even had an encounter with Mgr. Ralph Houk on the train after a game. Ryne smashed Houk's cigar into his face, and Houk, a tough Marine, countered with a punch to Ryne's face. He conquered his addiction in his post-career days and became an addiction counselor for foundations and hospitals, even speaking to players about the dangers of alcohol.

I never thought about it, but it's become increasingly evident as I'm writing this book that Richie Ashburn was right when he said,

"Pitchers are in a world of their own." Not only in my research but also in my own career. I find it incredible that I roomed with one of the two heaviest thinkers on analytics in baseball. One was Mike Marshall, and the other player was Trevor Bauer.

Two other unforgettable pitcher teammates that have provided me with a lifetime of memories were Bob Walz (Denver) and Al Schroll (Houston). They were free-spirit individuals, keeping the players loose for the long grind of a baseball season. I think pitchers have too much time to *think*: pitching every fourth or fifth day for starters, and relief pitchers whenever needed. Out in the bullpen, there is a lot of down time. Funny things happen in bullpens: lots of conversation, laughter, pranks, etc. Back in the 1960s the N.Y. Mets even had a vegetable garden in its Shea Stadium pen. I mentioned Mickey McDermott in another chapter – another pitcher.

I almost forgot a pitcher I played with at Little Rock, Arkansas – Robert Bo Belinsky. Bo was a good pool player. I was okay at pool and enjoyed his company occasionally before going to the ballpark. Bo eventually played with the Los Angeles Angels and even pitched a no-hitter. Bo was a pool hustler, heavy drinker, and a playboy. While in Los Angeles, he dated Mamie Van Doren, Ann-Margret, Tina Louise, Juliet Prowse, and Connie Stevens. He married Jo Collins.

His post-career life was very sad. My recollection of Bo as a teammate was completely opposite his later and post-career experiences. I suppose his fame, Hollywood good looks, Hollywood acquaintances, and alcohol took a toll on this otherwise regular guy. Bo and Jo Collins eventually divorced He moved to Hawaii and met his wife to be – Jane Weyerhaeuser, heiress to the Weyerhaeuser Paper fortune. They eventually divorced.

Gene Mauch, a brilliant, fiery manager, said, "I wish I had a thousand guys with his arm and none with his head."[10] I recall Mauch's managerial ability while playing for Denver and Houston vs. Mauch's Minneapolis team. I find it incredible that my baseball career crossed paths with so many iconic personalities mentioned in this book-writing venture. I also am saddened to hear of the post-career misfortunes of people that I have known. Belinsky battled bladder cancer before his death from a heart attack at age sixty-four. R.I.P., Bo!

While in Lynchburg, Virginia, one of our pitchers from Pennsylvania had gone to high school with Joe Namath. We were in Birmingham, Alabama, for a four-game series, and Joe visited his old schoolmate. I was invited to join them for golf but declined. I always regretted not going. I heard it was a ball. Just as well, I might have missed the game. Richie's quote on pitchers certainly rings true.

Let's talk about relief pitchers. The analytical era has moved this group to the forefront, much to the dismay of many fans. This analytical era stresses 27 outs, no matter how you get them. Out-getting is the next great strategy. This rethinks the role of starters, middle relievers, and closers.

---

[10] Bo Belinsky – https://sabr.org/bioproj/person/353987ab

Today, starting pitchers do less. Five or six innings are the norm, leading to a parade of relief pitchers. Eight-man bullpens are common. Complete games are obsolete. Five starters are not enough, six are needed. Houston had seven in 2018. Starters are more important in October when only three or four per series are needed.[11] With computer analytics, relief pitchers are coming in more frequently than ever. A reliever could be performing very well, but if computer analytics data calls for another pitcher vs. a particular hitter, the computer trumps reason and performance.

Relief pitchers coming in for one hitter is now fairly common. This will change in 2020 with a new rule change. Relief pitchers must face a minimum of three hitters or completion of the half inning. Pitch counts are now in vogue – to the extreme. One hundred seems to be the magic number. Tune into any MLB game, and the announcer is frequently found reciting the number of thrown pitches by a struggling pitcher, as early as the first or second inning. One bad inning almost guarantees a relief pitcher later in the game. Close to 100 pitches, and you're gone.

Minor League pitchers are also on pitch counts: sometimes 65-75 pitches. Wimpy? I'm not sure, however, the young minor league arms are not being conditioned for longer appearances in preparation for MLB. Pretty soon, we will have 45-man rosters to accommodate more relief pitchers.

---

[11] https://www.usatoday.com/story/sports/mlb/2018/03/21/mlb-bullpenning-rotation-pitching-staff

In the course of my research, I stumbled upon an interesting column by Rob Arthur, a baseball columnist for Five Thirty Eight,[12] a sports blog. The subject was the MLB disabled list. For years, the DL was fifteen days. In 2017 it became ten days. Players who were unable to perform due to injury were placed on the DL list, and a replacement player took his roster spot. This created an opening for a little dishonesty. Smart teams could look ahead at the schedule, use an open date, and "disable" a fifth starting pitcher, and then skip his spot in the rotation, call up a reliever from AAA, and fill the roster space. If the starter is needed again, the AAA player is sent back. Was the starter really injured? Needed some rest? "Ten days become **better** than fifteen!"[13] Of course, there is no cheating in baseball.

Casey Stengel in 1953

[12] https://fivethirtyeight.com/features/howthedodgers...

[13] Ibid.

CHAPTER SEVEN

Pitching / Analytics / Injuries

When they operated, I told them to put in a Koufax fastball. They did – but it was Mrs. Koufax's.
- Tommy John

Let's examine some consequences of this analytical era. In today's quest for increased velocity, players at a young age are risking elbow and shoulder injuries. Players at the high school level and some even earlier are watching MLB pitchers, attending special camps, and attempting to throw harder, perhaps, than their limitations. Oftentimes, their parents push them to achieve college scholarships and some even direct them toward professional contracts. Increased specialization (baseball year-round) deprives players of needed rest.

So, as usual, what we have are many different opinions and many studies, none of which has much empirical evidence on either side. I'll proceed to give you some examples of opinions and various studies and let you be the judge.

My roommate, Mike Marshall, took his show on the road after retirement. Dr. Mike advocated a delivery featuring an exaggerated pronation of the arm. He figured this would put less stress on the elbow. Dr. Glenn Fleisig largely debunked Mike's theory. In 2014 Dr. Fleisig was the research director of ASM I, American Sports Medical Institute and leader in baseball pitching biomechanics.[1]

Dr. Fleisig was involved in such studies as elbow and arm injuries, TJS: Tommy John Surgery and sport specialization. He conducted studies and reached conclusions. Tommy John was a famous NY Yankees pitcher who suffered a severe elbow injury, UCL – Ulnar Collateral Ligament.[2] It figured to be a career-ending injury, but Tommy made a successful recovery. Hence, immortal recognition. This led to a countless number of articles and studies on causes, myths, and prevention of elbow and arm injuries in baseball. Dr. Fleisig drew some conclusions:[3] sport specialization, i.e., year-round play resulting in overuse, limited rest, and high velocity goals. Although TJS has an 80 percent success rate, it is a myth that you are stronger following the surgery. Maybe it was because you are forced to rest from overuse? I'll offer some

---

[1] drg/ennfieisigbaseballinjuries/Sloansportsconfereence/mitnews

[2] https://www.mlb.com/cwt4/why-is-it-called-tommy-john-surgery

[3] https://www.sloansportsconference.com/mit_news/ga-dr-glen-flesig-on-tommy-john-surgeryprevention-and-myths/...

interesting TJS observations. Good news: 80-90 percent of Major Leaguers make it back to the Majors. For those who had two TJS's, the comeback was not at their previous level of performance. Johnny Venters, Washington Nationals pitcher, is the first to make it back to the Majors after three TJS injuries.[4]

So Dr. Mike took a group of his "students" for Dr. Fleisig to observe. He put Dr. Mike's theories to test, and the answers indicated that his pupils' unorthodox deliveries would not conclusively reduce elbow injuries and produce far less velocity.[5] My roommate was not very happy. Mike fired back a very lengthy counterpoint letter to Dr. Fleisig, to no avail.[6] It was the longest and most technical reply imaginable. Mike, not one to hold back any opinions, made unflattering references to him and his associates for their work and insinuated low interest in protecting young arms.

If Mike's personality had been less abrasive and his presentation less intolerant of opposing viewpoints, his audience might have been more attentive. No way! No one liked him, other than myself. Every article I've ever read expressed disdain for Mike. It's a shame. I suppose Dr. Mike would be the antithesis in

---

[4] Ibid.

[5] https://www.drivelinebaseball.com/2011/10/reviewing-asmis-biomechanical-analysis...

[6] https://w.w.w.drmikemarshall.com/myevaluationoftheAmericanSports MedicineInstitutesBio...

this chapter. Iron Mike, winning the 1974 Cy Young Award, pitched in 106 games, 208 innings. All in relief.[7]

Let's examine some interesting theories and facts related to pitching and potential arm injuries. I'll list these in no particular order, just for your information. Some may even reappear in subsequent chapters, particularly in the Interview chapter.

Weighted balls, wrist weights, PlyoCare balls, Motus sleeves, javelins, and more are training tools. Driveline and other training facilities use these tools which are also available to the public.[8] It has developed into a money-making machine. Some high schools purchase the equipment which, under the proper supervision, can be helpful.

On weighted baseballs, Eric Cressey, president and co-founder of Cressey Sport Performance, offered some sound advice mainly for professional, college, and advanced high school players.[9] Some of his recommendations on use of weighted balls were: "not for use off the pitching mound, or long toss – limit toss six to eight feet away." "Don't play catch. Throw the ball, walk, pick it up. Use 7-11 ounce range!"

I came across a very interesting study on pitching injuries. It covered different age groups: Little League, high school and college.

---

[7] https://callforthepen.com/2016/11/06/ios-angeles-dodgers-history-mikemarshall-wins-cy-young-award

[8] https://wwwgoogle.com/search?q=drivelinebaseball+training+tools&source=792biw...

[9] ericcressey.com/Tag/weighted-baseballs-safe...

Between 2006 and 2010 Johna Register-Mihalik, a postdoctoral research associate in the Department of Exercise and Sports Science in the College of Arts and Sciences, conducted a five-year study of pitching injuries. Her team included Fred Mueller at UNC, Stephen Marshall at UNC Gillings School, and Barry Goldberg at Yale. Little League Baseball also participated.[10] They surveyed thousands of players, with Mihalik collecting and analyzing the data. I'll highlight some of the myths and facts exposed.

Little League pitchers who threw curves didn't get hurt any more than those that didn't. Curveballs put torque on the elbow. Sliders are faster and three times the risk for injury. Perplexing discovery: Kids who didn't throw curves or sliders still got hurt. Culprits: (1) High pitch counts and pitching too often. Leagues using pitch counts had a 50 percent lower risk of injury. It seems like pitching too often can be harmful, especially for those pitchers who, in addition to playing in a league, also play for a travel team, creating possible overuse of the arm, to say nothing about the added expense of such teams. College scholarships are obviously a motivation in most cases. (2) "High School pitchers were double the risk of Little League pitchers for arm problems and college pitchers double that of high school pitchers." (3) "60% of college pitchers reported taking pain relievers in order to pitch through elbow or

---

[10] https://college.unc.edu/2011/10/curveballs-sliders-and-pitch-counts-surviving-life-as-a-pitch...

shoulder pain." "Over 80% of college pitchers reported pitching when their arms were tired."[11]

An interesting sidebar discussion is the practice of long tossing, popularized by none other than Trevor Bauer. He stretches his arm out by throwing distances of 300 to 400 feet, three to five times a week. Most coaches frown on this practice, but Bauer enjoys it. I can relate to this from personal experiences I had during my playing career. Every spring training, without fail, I would develop a sore arm. Living in New Jersey, with cold winters, despite throwing in gymnasiums prior to spring training, it wasn't enough. I quickly discovered that I could stretch my shoulder into shape via long toss. Trevor Bauer would have been impressed.

Living up to his reputation for providing unexpected events, Bauer was involved in a classic incident on July 28, 2019. Bauer was on the mound for the Cleveland Indians vs. the Kansas City Royals. Bauer was having a frustrating inning and asked the umpire for a new ball. Meanwhile, Manager Terry Francona came out of the dugout to take Bauer out of the game. Bauer saw Francona coming and turned toward centerfield, throwing the ball over the fence, a 350-foot toss. He later apologized, saying he was frustrated and meant no disrespect toward Francona!

I find these studies to be very interesting. If I could choose one word to summarize this chapter, it would be overuse.

---

[11] Ibid.

CHAPTER EIGHT

Hitting / Analytics

> It's a round ball and a round bat, and you got to hit it square.
>
> - Pete Rose

Before getting into hitting analytics (some might call it "launching"), I thought it would be timely to list some of the great hitters I played with and against during my eleven-year professional baseball career. In my opinion, Ted Williams was the best left-handed hitter ever. The best left-handed hitter I played with was Billy Williams while at Houston – AAA – American Association. Opposing players stopped what they were doing when Billy was taking batting practice. Number 1, by far. Teammate Ron Santo was also outstanding. Both are Hall of Fame members. Gordon Windhorn, Denver – AAA – American Association, had great techniques. Gordon played with the Dodgers the following year. Others would include Deacon Jones (not the NFL player), Don Buford, and Russ Snyder.

Opposing hitters who were memorable would include Carl Yastrzemski, Pete Rose, Mickey Mantle, Ernie Banks, and Brooks Robinson. The player who hit the hardest ball imaginable was Mickey Mantle. Prior to signing with the Yankees, I worked out in Yankee Stadium right up to game time. During batting practice, while at shortstop, Mantle hit grounders in the hole between short and third that warranted only a look. Fielding it would have been futile.

A reasonable question to ask is how all of these great hitters, some single hitters like Pete Rose, others power hitters like Mickey Mantle, achieved so much in the pre- analytical era. As I stated in my poem in the beginning of the book, Pete Rose said, "I couldn't teach hitting today." Analytic proponents now ridicule Rose's emphasis on hitting *down* on the ball. Launching is now in vogue, and we will closely examine it in this chapter.

Power hitters were hitting their home runs by utilizing the theories of their era: hitting down on the ball (which in reality is a level swing). Analytic experts build a strong case for their theories. They argue that hitters THINK that they are hitting down on the ball, but they produce studies that show a slight uppercut.[1] They claim videos show that even Babe Ruth had a launch or slight uppercut swing. I was always under the impression that hard-hit grounders and line drives were sought-after objectives. Analytic proponents dispute that by claiming hard-hit grounders are outs, particularly if the infielders are shifted and playing deep, in most cases on the

[1] https://www.famousbaseballplayers.net/baberuthswing.html...

outfield grass. Shifting will be covered in detail in a later chapter. Hard to argue with their computer data, but teaching this swing could have negative consequences. It might be of some benefit – a few more home runs. It might hurt others – more strikeouts and weak fly balls brought on by an all-or-nothing approach.

Not to be outdone by their analytic nemesis, pitchers and hitters are seeking to establish their own analytic quest. In fact, hitters are habituating some of the same training facilities utilized by pitchers in the off-season. Kyle Boddy's Driveline Baseball is one such facility. Like pitchers, hitters pay for evaluations of physical and baseball skills. Various devices, such as Blast Sensors, PlyoCare balls, and K-vests measure skill levels. A batting cage provides the setting. Blast sensors are attached to the knob of the bat. The sensor measures bat speed, attack angle, and time-to-contact.[2]

Standard bat speed = 74.2 mph

Hand speed = 23 mph

Attack angle = 12 degrees

Time-to-contact = 14 seconds

Basically, you hit a Plyo, a sand-filled, weighted training ball which deforms on impact. It's teed up to provide feedback on quality of contact. The also wear K-vests (biofeedback), costing ($5,500), to measure hip, arm, hand, and bat speed. Four small

[2] https://www.drivelinebaseball.com/2019/05/debunking-bat-speed-myths...

wireless sensors capture speed, direction, acceleration, and deceleration of hitters' major movements: (1) attached to batting glove on lead-hand, (2) strapped to upper arm, (3) hangs on a harness worn around chest, (4) clipped to belt-like loop at pelvis.[3] Get the picture? I didn't realize all of this was going on behind the scenes. Amateurs and professional athletes are striving to get better. My immediate thought was admiration for this dedication. Proponents for all these analytical methods are quick to cite major improvements in MLB students' performance. I'll list some players shortly in this chapter who have improved their performance.

From my own professional player experience, I'm not completely sold. The data is certainly available for players to work on their weaknesses. Execution in competition is the ultimate goal, but *everyone* is different. Once again, will it work for everyone? The analytic era gurus enjoy using small samplings of pitching and hitting success stories to solidify their theories. Like golf, robotic practice and theories will not get you on the Professional Golf Tour.

Another training facility named Ball Yard, located in Northridge, California, is Doug Latta's headquarters.[4] It is low tech compared to Driveline, featuring one black and white standard definition camera. Latta played baseball in college and has no MLB affiliation. Latta doesn't want to inundate hitters with angles and

---

[3] https://www.k-motion.com/k-coach/kbaseball...

[4] https://blogs.fangraphs.com/inside-the-ballyard-with-doug-latta...

exit speeds. He says, "hitting is all about balance."[5] His friendship with Marlon Byrd (N.Y. Mets) led to off-season sessions and improvement in Byrd's performance. Byrd convinced Jason Turner, a teammate now with the Dodgers, to change his techniques which led to vast improvement.[6]

Word was spreading. The fly ball revolution was on. Latta claims he never talks about launching. He says fly ball emphasis is "misunderstood." He says hard or soft ground balls are discouraged. Just hard fly balls over the fielder's head or in the gap. Of course, home runs and line drives over the fielder's head are O.K.[7] Are you as confused as I am? This kind of selective acceptance and quest for fewer ground balls is going to be difficult for hitters to learn and execute. I know Latta stresses balance. However, hitters have to be overthinking and favoring an uppercut-launching swing. Time will tell, but I don't foresee a large sampling of player success. In my opinion, it may work for some but not all. Despite my humble opinion, the fly ball revolution is spreading. Young and old are accepting it. In 2014 Joe Maddon, Tampa Bay manager, said, "Offense is going south. Everything – data, video, all information, benefits pitching and defense."[8]

---

[5] Ibid

[6] Ibid

[7] Ibid

[8] https://www.mlb.com/rays>news>joe-maddon-rays-searchingforoffense...

Lost in all of this high-tech analytical movement is the elimination of small ball tactics. I've talked about it before. A mixture of the old and the new might be worthy of consideration. Man on second, nobody out, is a prime example. A chapter will be devoted to this very topic. Measurement is a key word found throughout analytical research. They collect data, feed it into a computer, and utilize it. I suppose a hypothetical can't be measured. If it could, I would love to see a study on how many possible runs in a season are lost by not advancing the runner to third. It's food for thought, interesting nevertheless.

Let's take a break from the heavy analytical research with some interesting hitting tidbits, in no particular order. On short players: Baseball America and scouts missed out on Jose Altuve's potential. They were looking for size vs. "strike zone management." Altuve is 5'6"[9] Some other short players: Fred Patek 5'4", Joe Morgan 5'7". I played against Patek in the Minors. Then we have Eddie Gaedel at 3'7". Yes, he was signed to a one-day contract by St. Louis Browns' owner Bill Veeck. He pinch hit, walked on four consecutive pitches, and was replaced by a pinch runner. It was 1951, St. Louis vs. Detroit. Veeck was well known for his baseball promotions.[10]

More short player facts: In 2018 Cleveland had two players: Francisco Lindor, 5'11" and Jose Ramirez, 5'9". Lindor hit 38 home

---

[9] Baseball America/ShortPlayers-Altuve,Patek.../Eddie Gaedel info-1951,Veeck

[10] Ibid

runs, and Ramirez hit 39. In 462 seasons, 178 different players hit 38 or more homers. In 46 seasons, 22 players 5'11" or shorter hit 38 or more homers.[11]

Stride tutor: David Gallagher-invented a plastic chain and Velcro attachment to prevent overstriding. Branch Rickey previously used a shot putter's guardrail to cure the same problem. Result – sprained ankles.[12] University of Iowa Coach Pete Lauritson invented a "Great wall of ground ball prevention." It was a ring of screens around the infield, encouraging hitters to *aim up*.[13]

I recently reflected on the vast amount of research material I've absorbed in writing this book: books, magazine articles, various guides on analytics, and numerous blogs on the internet. Analytics in pitching, hitting, and player development are dominant topics, with pitching at the forefront. Rightfully so, with pitching playing the most important role in baseball. As I'm writing this chapter on analytical hitting, I'm curious as to where ground zero took place. Does it exist? Is it just analytical theories made popular by the recent success of the Houston Astros? I thought of the book *Moneyball* and quickly dismissed it. *Moneyball* could claim rights to fostering today's analytics in player development. These questions need to be discussed in order to fully understand this analytical hitting craze.

---

[11] Ben Lindbergh/ Travis Sawchik, The MVP Machine, 257

[12] en.m.wikipedia.org>Dave_Gallagher

[13] twinsdaily.com>topic>28631-article...

Baseball has had its share of excellent hitting instructors. Opposing theories and viewpoints are common. From my viewpoint as a former professional player, this is not surprising, as hitting a baseball is one of the most difficult tasks in sports. The time period of my career was 1956-1967. Charley Lau had an eleven-year MLB career as a player and thirteen years as a coach. Charley was a well-respected hitting coach in that era, with many players utilizing his techniques. Charley espoused a balanced stance, rhythm, and hitting through the ball

Hitting through the ball actually incorporates an older technique used in the 1940s. It was a "belly button" principle credited to Paul Waner of the Pittsburg Pirates, ensuring that when you hit through the ball, your middle would be facing the pitcher. Paul said: "Throw your belly button at the pitcher." Ted Williams agreed: "You hit with your hips."[14] Paul was nicknamed Big Poison. His younger brother Lloyd was called Little Poison. They became the second brother combination to be elected to the MLB Hall of Fame. The other combination: Harry and George Wright who played in the late 1800s.

With the old theory of hitting down on the ball not adhered to now, hitters are trying to perfect a launching swing, with a launch angle between 26-30 degrees. Pitchers try to counteract this. Sinker ball pitchers throwing at 95-100 mph and hitters trying to hit the

---

[14] Googlepaulwanerbaseballbellybutton/books.google.com/thebaseball/ Coaching Bible-page 134

bottom of the ball is very difficult. Other pitchers try to throw high above the "launch angle." All this going on, and pitchers' needing to command or control the ball, have led to an increased risk for hitters. Aaron Judge was out for seven weeks, as a prime example. Hitters can't dive as much now. Altuve, a great hitter with a dive-like style, makes one wonder why he isn't thrown at more often. His style and attitude make him a prime candidate for head hunters.

Often overlooked and rarely mentioned is the difficulty in practicing these analytical hitting theories. Ordinary batting practice will not provide actual game conditions. Usually, batting practice pitchers will throw with much less velocity and very few breaking balls. Major League teams actually employ batting practice pitchers. Minor League teams (with less money) usually use an extra infielder or outfielder. Forget about pitching machines, even those that are capable of throwing breaking balls and decent velocity. I used to hate pitching machines. Some had a chute from which a ball would eject. Anticipation and timing were dominant. The mechanical arm type was better but still uncomfortable.

Finally, I'll finish with some research material that strikes home in regard to my personal baseball career. A quote claiming, "balls in the air to the pull-side are best." It went on to say, "Yet, pulling the ball has been discouraged for decades."

Pulling the ball is rare. Best hitters can do it well. Pulling is never taught. *Never.* Always go to the opposite field. The final quote really got my attention. "Amateurs suck at pulling the ball."[15] I reflected on my interview with Sam Tropiano when we were discussing hitting. He said, "pulling the ball is a good trait. Lots of hitters can't pull."

In my previous book, *Dugouts, Icons And Dreams*, I discussed hitting and pulling the ball in particular. I'll repeat it here, as I feel it represents different theories on hitting. I always considered myself a good hitter as an amateur yet had difficulty demonstrating this in my professional career, particularly as I moved up to a higher level. The reason: pulling the ball to an excess. I watched teammates compile higher batting averages than I by slapping the ball here or there.

While playing for Houston – AAA, I came out early before the game for extra hitting. Rogers Hornsby, the great MLB Hall of Fame player, was in town as a roving hitting instructor. Houston was a Chicago Cubs affiliate. The Yankees still owned me, however on loan to Houston. He watched from behind the batting cage, as I was spraying the ball to all fields. He told me "Don't change a thing." At game time, I would revert to pulling the ball. Not every time but enough to penalize myself. Of course trying to correct this became more difficult in AAA. My point is: A perceived strength (pulling) became a weakness in a high-level setting. I was hitting the ball harder than my teammates were, with less success. Just a little digression on theories and opinions, etc. In my case, some

---

[15] Ben Lindbergh/ Travis Sawchik, The MVP Machinew,257

opposite field hitting instruction at an earlier age would have been very beneficial.

I came across an interesting quote on analytical hitting that will conclude this chapter. It was provided by Driveline Hitting Director Jason Ochart, a kinesiology, biomechanics expert: "lot of **gray** area in hitting compared to pitching, in Analytics."

Despite that comment, Ochart has plenty of sophisticated analytical theories if the reader cares to pursue his technical opinions. The Phillies hired Ochart in 2018 as their Minor League hitting director.[16]

Houston (above) in 1960, he played with future Hall of Famer Billy Williams

[16] https://wwwdrivelinebaseball.com/2016/10 coaching-hitting-mwchanics...

CHAPTER NINE

Player Development

To change and improve are two different things.
- German proverb

Luck! I've heard many quotes on luck. "I'd rather be lucky than good." "Luck is the residue of design." These are two of my favorites. However it is defined, I consider my introduction to professional baseball an event that in retrospect can be called just luck.

Instead of going all in on analytics, teams should also think of alternative player development possibilities. Thus, I consider myself very fortunate to have received top-notch instruction from the very beginning of my New York Yankees career. I was invited to a special instruction camp in St. Petersburg, Florida, prior to the regular spring training at another site. It also overlapped the Yankees Major League training camp. I'll mention the all-star instruction staff in my chapter on double plays. Expert instructors taught us the Yankee way, and then we went to our assigned team for an extended spring training and prepared for the coming season. You better yourself through competition. When I was playing basketball, I wanted to play against good players in game situations where I formed winning habits.

I find it incredible that in the year 2020, MLB teams – the Houston Astros, in particular – are searching for player development ideas that I experienced in the late 1950s. In this analytical era, teams are downsizing their farm system. Houston is going from nine teams to seven.[1] MLB is considering eliminating lower classifications and keeping only A, AA, and AAA. Houston and other copycat organizations plan to train their entry-level prospects at their Minor League spring training facility. They figure they can instill the analytical data in their players better in this atmosphere than in actual *league* play.[2] This Minor League contraction is at the expense of long-time faithful Minor League cities. I think it is a mistake on many counts. Players and fans will suffer. I'll explain the fans dilemma in a later chapter: Fans!

Force feeding entry-level prospects with new analytical theories and data, while valuable in itself, seems incomplete. Should the data be tested? Tested in competition? By competition, I don't mean intra-squad games. By eliminating lower leagues, where most of these entry-level prospects would be assigned, true

---

[1] ballparkdigest.com/ more details emerge...

[2] Ibid

competition is lacking. If you don't care about instilling winning and team values, then I rest my case.

On second thought, before I rest my case, let's not forget some extraneous factors involved here. Money and Politics. MLB is playing politics under the guise of expense. MLB wants franchise owners to contribute more money in their shared expense arrangement for the right to be an affiliate of a MLB club. Eliminating lower Minor League franchises and an entire league would achieve this purpose. The Houston Astros farm club contraction strengthens MLB's position. Fans and baseball performance are ignored. Prime prospects will start in higher classifications and arrive in the big leagues sooner than normal. Instead of making their mistakes in the low minors, they will make them in the majors. Now I'll rest my case.

In 2013 *Moneyball* and Billy Beane's success was giving way to Bill James and his Sabermetrics movement and search for objective knowledge about baseball. In 2015 MLB introduced Statcast which supplanted PITCHf/x and HITf/x systems. Statcast, with its cameras and radar, was recording pitch speed, velocity, and trajectory of every hit ball in every big league park. Trackman monitored all thirty Major League teams.[3] Now data attempts to show what makes players *better.* Sabermetric reformers, NARPS, would now clash with traditional thinkers. NARPS is a phrase coined by New York Sports Host Boomer Esiason, a former NFL

---

[3] fivethirtyeight.com 2015 pitchf/xsystems/Trackmanall30teams...

quarterback. The morning show is called Boomer and Gio on WFAN, NY (Gio – Gregg Giannotti). NARP stands for Non-Athletic Regular Person. Mutual ignorance polarizes relationships – Traditional vs. NARPS. Heart and grit, traditional traits, were countered by Analytical Era quotes, such as "Grit is an analytical trait for *more practice*."

Conduits were now being hired. Gabe Kapler, the fired Phillies' manager, being a prime example. Kapler had a long MLB career and was a staunch analytic supporter. Fans disliked him. Press conferences were painful to watch. The Phillies fired him and the pitching coach. While it's too early to judge, new manager Joe Girardi and pitching coach Jason Price appear to be good hires.

Player development is changing. Staffs are increasing. In 2011 the Houston Astros had 51, in 2018 – 78. The New York Yankees in 2018 had 102 player development staff members. NARPS are taking over. The Astros downsized their farm teams from nine to seven. Philosophies have changed![4] Branch Rickey used to say, "Out of quantity comes quality." The Astros say, "Out of quantification comes quality."[5]

By downsizing, the Astros feel they can train and evaluate better, spending time on more promising players. Former Astro personnel are flooding MLB and 20 percent are now managers and

---

[4] https://www.theringer.com/mlb/2019/6/3/mvpmachine-how-houston-astros-became...

[5] Ibid

coaches for other teams. It remains to be seen how the cheating scandal will affect the Astros reputation. Get the drift? The Houston Astros' success has fostered an outbreak in baseball of increased analytical aspirations. Player development, technology, copycat organizations, and companies for profit are at the forefront.

Baseball is becoming more expensive. Lower income parents can't afford funding for instruction camps and even travel team expenses. Famous places like Driveline are too expensive. Systems like Trackman are expensive, even for teams. In 2016 MLB and USA Baseball sponsored events by invitation only for high school players.[6] Thus rushing data on prospects to sign them puts too much emphasis on showcasing.

MLB has morphed into a younger and stat-minded group. General managers are male, white, and Ivy League. Tampa Bay in 2019 had a Stathead coach – Jonathan Erlichman – as its director of analytics.

Some points to ponder:

General Managers

Former MLB Players	Minor Leaguers	Ivy Leaguers
1980's - 44%	1980's - 67%	2010 - 40%
2010 - 2%	2010 - 2%	1970 - 1990s - 3%[7]

---

[6] https://www.mlb.com/news/mlb-usa-baseball-prospect-development-pipeline...

[7] Baseball Prospectus>news>article?27861/outta-left-field...Dustin Palmateer

Along with analytics, player development changes have included sophisticated weight-training methods. In 2016 Boston Biomotion (BB),[8] featured Robot-like equipment, resistance, etc. In 2018 the Dodgers became the first MLB team to partner with BB. They installed a Proteus system. The system tracks everything and claims it "alters and improves the way athletes train and rehab." It features sophisticated weight-training methods. A far cry from my era, when weightlifting, etc., was discouraged as harmful for baseball. The BB system is costly, and time will tell its success.

Player development is an important phase of baseball. With prejudice, I still think more time should be spent on teaching fundamentals. I see too many good MLB players making mistakes. I want to see studies on the value of these fundamentals being ignored. I'll cover this in my Double Play chapter.

The analytical proponents brag about measuring in all of my research findings. Measuring is a key word. Before you measure the success of something, fundamentally correct principles must be established. What good is measuring something that is fundamentally wrong? Therefore, I'll repeat my call for emphasizing correct fundamentals. Science is great. In baseball, the theme for player development should be Back to Basics.

Since I'm writing this in real time, it might be apropos to provide an update on the Covid-19 pandemic and its effect on MLB. July

---

[8] https://wwwsportsbusinessdaily.com/Daily/issues/2018/12/13/Franchises/Dodgers...

2020 is fast approaching and still no baseball season. Forget about the Minor Leagues this season. Of course, the virus situation transcends baseball, but life goes on, and hopefully baseball will return soon with some sort of normalcy. Throughout this pandemic, MLB and the Players Union have been wrangling back and forth over countless proposals. Starting dates for another spring training, season opening dates, length of season, spectators, player safety and salaries, playoff and World Series dates are major concerns. Meanwhile, the threat of a 2021 strike looms heavily over MLB and the Players Union. Their contract agreement is up next year, and negotiations are stalled as usual. Fans are hardly in the mood for another strike. It's really a bad time for all major sports. They always seem to bounce back, but attendance figures will surely suffer.

NEW YORK YANKEES
SPRING TRAINING CAMP - 1957

Front Row, seated from left: *3rd - BILL DAVIDSON*

Middle Row, seated from left: *2nd - Bill Dickey, 3rd - Ralph Houk, 4th - Eddie Lopat, 5th - Casey Stengel, 6th - Johnny Neun, 7th - Frank Crosetti*

Back Row, standing from left: *1st - Marv Thorneberry, 3rd - Tony Kubek, 4th - Deron Johnson*

Yankee spring training – 1957

YANKEES – When Billy Davidson signed with the New York Yankees, he got to sit in front of Bill Dickey, a future Hall of Famer, in the 1957 rookie camp team picture.

CHAPTER TEN

Shifting / Pros and Cons

The way these clubs shift against Ted Williams, I can't understand how he can be so stupid not to accept the challenge to him and hit to left field.
- Ty Cobb

After examining analytical changes and developments in two of the major categories: pitching and hitting, let's take a breather. Let's talk defense. Other than shifting, defense gets very little attention in the overall modern or analytical era. In the long run, I think it could be a mistake. In the next few chapters, I will attempt to disprove some defensive theories. Restoring the importance of some key traditional elements, together with some analytical additions, might satisfy some lost fans and also increase chances for added victories during the season. Playoffs? World Series? Who knows?

In no particular order, I'll list some shifting facts compiled from my playing experience and books and articles I've read in my research efforts. With the exception of a few earlier shifts, shifting probably started in 1946, when Cleveland Indians Player and Manager Lou Boudreau employed a radical shift on Boston Red Sox outfielder Ted Williams. Ted later said that he tried to beat the shift but decided he wasn't going to ruin his swing for a few hits to left field. It was called the Boudreau Shift, later changed to the Ted Williams Shift.[1] According to BIS (Baseball Info Solutions), 2,463 shifts were made on batted balls in 2010. By 2016, the total was 28,130. Incredible![2]

Some fans don't like the shifts. It has even captured Commissioner Rob Manfred's attention. If attendance figures diminish, expect some changes. That's the way it works. It's been said that changes favor the pitchers and fielders. I say no. It *could* actually help the hitters. When I see all the shifting going on with infielders out of position to execute a double play, for instance, it confounds me. That, together with other obvious technique mistakes these Major League shortstops and second basemen are making, and listening to announcers and experts blaming the wrong player for the mistakes is inexcusable. These are good players and athletes, but they lack proper techniques. It doesn't speak well of Major League infield instructors. It's costing teams lots of runs and games. I will expound on this in my Double Play chapter.

---

[1] www.cbssports.com just because...

[2] https://sportsinfosolutionsblog.com>whatis...

Shift proponents might counter with, "Won't shifting, creating outs instead of hits, cancel out games lost from not adhering to some *traditional* methods?" My answer is no. So could the analytical data be skewed? Are infielders playing too deep, taking them out of *potential* double play opportunities? How about slow-hit balls, topped balls, swinging bunts? Infielders are playing on the outfield grass. By the time they field the ball, the runner is safe.

One other area of defense that the average fan is probably not aware of is framing. This practice has been going on throughout baseball history. Basically, it involves catchers and their ability to frame a pitch, making a pitch to a batter appear to be a strike when in reality it is a ball. Some catchers are much better at this art than others. In fact, this ability hasn't escaped the attention of analytical era proponents. It actually produces a measurable value.

Catchers are rated and assigned values to their respective teams. Brian McCann, Atlanta Braves catcher, was reported to be at the top of the framing class. Catchers are rated from the best to the worst. McCann was said to be worth 25+ runs per season.[3] Numbers are fed into a computer, and a favorable value can result in salary compensation and even selection to a team. Brian is now thought to have lost his edge a bit since coming out of retirement. His successors appear to be the following, with their run worth and team listed:[4]

[3] https://baseballsavant.mlb.com/catcher-framing=2019&team

[4] Ibid

Player	Team	Run Value
1- Austin Hedge	San Diego	20
2- Tyler Flowers	Atlanta	13
3- Yasmani Grandal	Chicago White Sox	13
4- Roberto Perez	Cleveland	12
5- Buster Posey	San Francisco	10
6- J.T. Realmuto	Philadelphia	8

I know umpires are aware of this deception; however, some catchers are so adept at this subtle skill that it is difficult to prove. Cheating? Perhaps, but analytical proponents will just call it a measurable value. Umpires retaliation? Time will tell.

My conclusion is that analytical shifting practice should not be used at the expense of traditional techniques. A blend of both can produce better results, more wins, and more championships.

CHAPTER ELEVEN

Man On Second / Nobody Out

Who's on first. What's on second. I don't know is on third.

Abbott & Costello

As I previously stated, this book is for the average fan. The title of this chapter focuses on a situation that occurs in just about every game. As a shortstop, this is one of my favorite topics. The opinion I'm going to offer epitomizes traditional strategy and questions analytical theories. To be sure, even though this chapter is about hitters' responsibilities, it is intermingled with defense.

In Chapter 10, Shifting, I discussed drawbacks. I'll take it a step farther and discuss the thought processes that are going on with the infielders, particularly the shortstop and second baseman. They love a force out situation, making their job much easier.

An example of a force out would be when a runner on first with second base unoccupied tries to advance to second on a ground ball. The fielder simply touches the bag, creating a force out. Man on second, nobody out – now their job is harder – no force out. Here the hitter has the advantage. Their job is to advance the runner on second to third. Now you have a man on third, with one out. A sacrifice fly, bunt, passed ball, error, a run scores.

I don't know how many games I have watched where the hitter fails in this situation. A ball hit to the first base side of the field, even a weak grounder or fly ball to right field, would advance the runner to third. The hitters are swinging for the fences and even flying out weakly to left field. Then you will have a man on second with one out. It's still no force out but a better situation.

Of course, the runner can score on a hit, but other possibilities open up. A walk puts runners on first and second with one out. You are back to a force out situation with less pressure on the fielders. Even if you don't get a double play, which you probably won't because shifting decreases your chances, you still can get a force out. Force outs and double plays win lots of games. On offense, moving a runner to third wins lots of games. Are these measurable situations? Traditional vs. analytical? Your choice.

Analytical proponents will counter with: We care only about getting twenty-seven outs, no matter how we get them. They are all in for doubles, triples, and home runs. This is surely not my way of thinking with 1,500 games under my belt. The frequency of this situation deserves more serious attention than today's game is providing.

I'll continue to keep baseball and the Covid-19 pandemic news up to date. It's now mid-July 2020. MLB and the Players Union finally settled on a shortened 60-game season. The Minor League season was cancelled. Many fans think MLB should have cancelled likewise. TV money was a major persuader.

Players are now undergoing spring training in their respective cities and home ballparks. Season opener: late July. No spectators. Cardboard cutouts will represent fans. Sound will be piped in. Some star players have already opted out. I predict more will follow. Perhaps the season will never start after all?

Repercussions abound. High school players have already missed their senior year. Minor League players have been released. Only the top-rated prospects remain (those that received more bonus money to sign). College players missed a season. Some colleges have already cancelled 2021 sport programs. All of this and the predicted 2021 strike over bargaining differences between MLB and the Players Union. Stay tuned.

CHAPTER TWELVE

CHASE UTLEY RULE

> "The base paths belonged to me, the runner. The rules give me the right. I always went into a bag full speed, feet first. I had sharp spikes on my shoes. If the baseman stood where he had no business to be and got hurt, that was his fault."
>
> - Ty Cobb

As a former shortstop in over 1,500 professional baseball games, one might think that I would favor this rule. Chase Utley was a second baseman for the Philadelphia Phillies and Los Angeles Dodgers. His famous takeout slide of New York Mets' shortstop Ruben Tejada in the 2015 National League Division Series was ruled intentional. He was suspended for two games. The suspension was later overturned.

I think it is ludicrous. It's the latest step in mollifying modern-day baseball. Chase Utley played hard. Unfortunately, Tejada suffered a broken leg. He probably never was the same player after recovery. I've seen videos of this slide a number of times. Admittedly, it was a very hard, aggressive slide. In a later chapter,

I will describe how Tejada made himself vulnerable to an injury that could have been avoided.

As a shortstop, I was taken out of a double play once. Surely, a world record if records were kept on such plays. This happened in a AA Southern League game in 1958, playing for New Orleans vs. Chattanooga, Tennessee. The late Bob Allison on first and I believe the late Hall of Fame outfielder, Harmon Killebrew, hitting. With Allison running on a hit-and-run play, the batter hit a hard grounder to our second baseman. Knowing Allison, a 240-pound, 6'4" former University of Kansas football player had a running start, I knew I would have to get rid of the ball instantly and would still get hit. Allison never slid, knocking me toward left field. I fortunately didn't get hurt, and we made the double play. This was all part of the game played back in the day.

The catchers rule exemplifies Major League Baseball changes. Fans don't want injuries, but there have to be other alternatives. I suppose Pete Rose's collision with catcher Ray Fosse, fracturing his shoulder, in the July 17, 1970 All Star game in Cincinnati in the twelfth inning epitomizes the rule changes in today's game.[1] Once again, I'm on Pete Rose's side. Ray was blocking the plate before he had the ball. All bets are off at that point. You either hit the catcher or risk injury to yourself. Catchers have protective equipment on and you don't. A broken leg or worse is conceivable, if sliding is your choice. Buster Posey's injury in May 2011, forcing

[1] MLB.com>news>pete-rose-collis...

him to miss the rest of the season, probably played an important role in the eventual rule change in 2014.

In my opinion, fans want to see action play. However, if a player intentionally tries to hurt someone, he should be penalized. A good, hard, clean slide is real baseball.

CHAPTER THIRTEEN

Double Plays / Measurable Value

"Baseball's Sad Lexicon:" A tribute to shortstop Joe Tinker, second baseman Johnny Evers and first baseman Frank Chance, Chicago Cub players in 1910 whose efforts helped win championships!

These are the saddest of possible words:
"Tinker to Evers to Chance."
Trio of bear cubs, and fleeter than birds,
Tinker and Evers and Chance.
Ruthlessly pricking our gonfalon bubble,
Making a Giant hit into a double-
Words that are heavy with nothing but trouble:
"Tinker to Evers to Chance."
- Franklin Pierce Adams

This is my favorite chapter. If there is one facet of baseball in which I can confidently claim to have expertise, it's the double play. Even the so-called analytical experts cannot challenge me for many reasons. First and foremost is the origin of this acquired knowledge. I was very fortunate to have been invited to a Special

Instruction Training Camp in the spring of 1957. This camp overlapped the regular New York Yankees Spring Training Camp in St. Petersburg, Florida. Casey Stengel oversaw the camp, and the staff included excellent coaches and instructors – Ralph Houk, Bill Dickey, Eddie Lopat, Frank Crosetti, and Johnny Neun, to name a few. The regular Yankee players arrived, including Mickey Mantle, Yogi Berra, Moose Skowron, Don Larsen, and others. It was a great way to start a career.

Frank Crosetti was in charge of the infielders. Genius, an overused word, but Frank was without question far ahead of his time. His complete thought process and methods have stood the test of time. They were simple but concise. I haven't come across all of his methods, even in my extensive research efforts. Some perhaps but not all. Certainly not in the MLB games I watch today.

I get angry when the analytical era proponents downplay the old traditional era style of baseball. They call it small ball. From this point forward, I'm going to rename it. Let's call it "smart ball." Proponents of analytics stress pitching and hitting, virtually ignoring the value of defense, with the exception of shifting. Pitching, with spin rate, spin axis, and so on, and hitting with launching, exit velocity, etc., are dominant. By the end of this chapter, I hope to prove defense, particularly the double play, is just as valuable in this modern era. I'll call it smart ball revisited. I'll stick to my stance, with full knowledge of the current fly ball quest.

Some of this subject is mentioned in my book *Dugouts, Icons And Dreams*. It is worth repeating here, in view of this book's subject, analytics. I watch and listen to announcers describing a play and blaming the wrong player for a botched double play. Major League players, many of them great athletes, are making mistakes in every game. Later in my career, playing in other organizations, I would have to explain the proper techniques to my new teammates for the benefit of the team. Otherwise, I envisioned a long season. All of this reinforces my appreciation of Frank Crosetti's talent. The Yankee Way. I marvel at his thought process, since no one else at that time or for that matter now executes his techniques properly. I'll explain in detail shortly.

So along comes the analytical age with their super computers manned in most cases by NARPS, dismissing smart ball. Before explaining Crosetti's methods, I must explain the premise of my counterpoint to the analytical proponents. The key words are measured value. This is key in most of my research on analytics in baseball. In my Shifting chapter, I mentioned various drawbacks. Shift proponents, however, will ignore those drawbacks, saying the shift will provide benefits. For the sake of simplicity, they assign a value to every batted ball; however, they ignore potential double plays. It's called a measured value which is assigned throughout analytics. Basically, it's just more data.

To make it simple, they feed the collected data into the computer, and it becomes the norm. This sounds good if you're counting pitch after pitch (pitch counts) and other measurable data. Here's the catch. On double plays, with infielders shifted out of position to make a double play and virtually all MLB infielders committing various mistakes and executing faulty techniques, a measurable value no longer exists. No norm. Therefore, there is no way to collect accurate data. Garbage in, garbage out!

Getting back to my earlier statement on how defense and double plays in particular are being ignored in the analytical era, I submit that their value is being undermined. Shifting and technique mistakes are costing more runs and more games lost than it appears. Double plays are ruled safe or out by a micro second. Unless all of the methods I suggest are executed properly, games will be lost during the course of a long season. I'll repeat: all the methods, not some.

I'll now reveal Frank Crosetti's instruction. I remember all details like it was yesterday. Six steps in all. Simple, yet ignored. Simple, yet I haven't seen them in print. Simple, yet not followed by MLB players. Execute five of the six steps; the runners are safe, no double play. It's that simple.

Frank's Six Steps

1. Get to the bag as fast as possible. No timing to get there as the ball arrives.

2. Chicken steps to slow you down if you arrive before the throw.

3. Not anticipating a good throw, be balanced and ready to go in any direction.

4. No reaching. Reaching out, favoring left or right side.

5. Throwing hand close to glove hand. Prevents wasted motion.

6. Short arm. Short, quick motion. No long, winding motion. Acquired through practice. Velocity not sacrificed.

In chapter eleven - Chase Utley Rule, I mentioned that I would describe how the NY Mets shortstop Ruben Tejada's injury could have been avoided. This chapter on double plays is the perfect opportunity to do so. Now that we know how to execute the double play, let's examine Tejada's unfortunate injury and how it could have been avoided. I've watched this many times in slow motion and have come to several conclusions. First and foremost, there was no way a double play was going to happen. The ball was hit over the second base bag, and the second baseman fielded it deep beyond the bag. At this point, the shortstop must act like a first baseman, stretching to receive the ball from the second baseman. Forget the double play. Be content with a force out. Instead, Tejada violated almost all of my aforementioned double play techniques. No chicken steps, reaching out flat footed, and doing a half pirouette 180 degree turn. It was an injury waiting to happen. Correctly done, Tejada would have had a vision of all the action in front of him and avoided the collision. His method assured the oncoming danger. You do those pirouette moves only with no runner on first base. My verdict: injury entirely avoidable.

Having played professional baseball for eleven years at a high level (AAA) at the most difficult position – shortstop, I feel qualified to offer drawbacks on both shifting and double plays. It puts me in a unique position – playing experience, with enough analytical knowledge to appreciate the principles involved.

Frank Crosetti's techniques helped me throughout my career. They helped me become part of a team that set the all-time double play record for organized baseball (Major and Minor Leagues). It was in New Orleans, Southern League in 1958. In 154 games, we had 241 double plays. No wonder the Yankees were winning so much in those days. So I know how much double plays contribute to a team's quest for wins.

I hope I explained this to my average fan readers. I'll point out other areas where analytic benefits and drawbacks are suspect. On double plays, I will not be challenged.

Pels Close Out Season Dropping Two to Chicks

Eleven Homers Blasted in Twin Bill

By BILL KEEFE

One more one-run reverse was added to the Pelicans astonishing record of "nose" defeats Sunday evening when the Memphis Chicks took both ends of the season's final doubleheader by 5 to 4 and 7 to 5.

Pushing all known records for home runs in one park was the total of 11 circuit clouts for the twin bill.

The biggest consulation the attendance of 240 paid enjoyed was the amazing completion of two double plays in the first game to give the Birds an all-time record of 238 for the season—16 more than a long-standing mark turned in by the Nashville Vols in 1952.

Pitcher Frank Baumann smacked a homer over the left field fence in the fourth to give the Chicks a 6 to 2 stranglehold on the contest, but in their half of the fourth the Pels took advantage of Baumann's wildness and, but for a brilliant catch by McCarthy of a terrific drive that Tresh would have put over the centerfield fence, the Pels most probably would have piled up more runs. Bill Davidson poled a long homer over the deep centerfield fence with two on — Hunt and Leja had walked — Baumann got out of the hole and was leading 6 to 5 as the fifth inning opened. Tony Asaro had homered in the first inning after Jack Reed had singled and that accounted for the Pels' first two runs.

In the opener Cereghino had the Chicks 4 to 3 after six innings and though the top half of the sixth was rocky for him, inasmuch as the Visitors loaded the bases with two down, but the big Pel pitcher came up with a grounder by McKee and retired the side.

Meanwhile Stablefeld had closed the gate on the Pels and turn defeat into victory for the Tribe.

FIRST GAME

Memphis—	AB	R	H	RBI
Tanner 3b	3	1	1	1
Frazier 2b	4	1	1	0
McCarthy cf	4	0	0	0
Dipippo 1b	4	0	2	1
Sczesny rf	3	1	1	0
Comolli c	3	1	2	1
Grote lf	2	0	1	1
McKee ss	3	1	1	1
Stablefeld p	2	0	1	0
a-Rivich	1	0	0	0
Slack p	0	0	0	0
Totals	29	5	10	5

NEW ORLEANS—	AB	R	H	RBI
Reed cf	3	0	0	0
Asaro 2b	3	1	2	0
Hunt rf	4	1	1	2
Leja 1b	3	1	2	1
Snyder lf	4	0	0	0
Tresh 3b	2	1	1	0
Davidson ss	3	0	2	1
North c	2	0	0	0
Utley p	0	0	0	0
Cereghino p	3	0	0	0
Totals	27	4	8	4

a—Grounded out for Stablefeld in 7th.

Davidson, Asaro and Leja; Asaro, Davidson and Leja. LOB-Memphis 7, New Orleans 7. 2B-Davidson, Asaro, Tresh, Dipippo. HR-Hunt, Comolli, McKee, Leja, Tanner. SB-Davidson. S-Tresh.

	IP	H	H	ER	BB	SO
Stbfld (W 8-10)	6	8	4	4	1	5
Slack	1	0	0	0	2	2
Crghn (L 9-16)	5⅔	10	5	5	4	2
Utley	⅓	0	0	0	0	0

WP-Cereghino, Stablefeld. U-Daugherty and Burns. T-1:45.

SECOND GAME

MEMPHIS—				
Tanner, 3b	3	1	1	2
Frazier, 2b	2	1	1	0
McCarthy, cf	4	0	2	1
Dipippo, 1b	4	0	0	0
Sczesny, rf	2	2	2	1
Grote, lf	3	1	2	2
McKee, ss	3	0	0	0
Rivich, c	3	0	0	0
Baumann, p	2	2	2	1
Totals	26	7	10	7

NEW ORLEANS—	AB	R	H	RBI
Reed, cf	3	1	1	0
Asaro 2b	3	1	1	2
Hunt, rf	2	1	0	0
Leja, 1b	1	1	0	0
Snyder, lf	3	0	0	0
Tresh, 3b	2	0	0	1
Davidson, ss	3	1	1	2
Maley, c	2	0	0	0
Utley p	0	0	0	0
a.Nardella	1	0	0	0
Henriksen, p	0	0	0	0
b-North	1	0	0	0
Yochim, p	0	0	0	0
Totals	21	5	3	5

a—Struck out for Utley in 3rd; b—Grounded out for Hendriksen in 4th.

(Called end 6th because of curfew.)

Score by innings:

Memphis	041	101—7
NEW ORLEANS	200	300—5

Summary: E-Maley, McKee. PO-A-Memphis 18-5, New Orleans 18-11. LOB-Memphis 6, New Orleans 2. 2B-McCarthey, Frazier HR-Asaro, Grote, Tanner, Sczesny, Baumann, Davidson. SB-Reed. S-Frazier. SF-Tresh.

The infielders are BILL DAVIDSON, shortstop; Tony Asaro, third base; Bob Maness, second base, and FRANK LEJA, first base.

ALL SET for their home debut is this 1958 edition of the Pelicans who'll do battle with Mobile tonight in City Park stadium. The outfielders packing their Louisville sluggers are, from left, RICHIE WINDLE, reserve outfielder; KEN HUNT, right field; JACK REED, center field, and RUSS SNYDER, left field.

CHAPTER FOURTEEN

Position Rankings / Hardest to Easiest

> An opinion which excites no opposition at all is not worth having!
>
> \- Marie Corelli

Just for a little diversion from analytics, I offer my opinion on position difficulty. This is based on my own professional baseball career. Have fun with your choices.

1. SHORTSTOP

I suppose I'm a little biased, having played shortstop my entire career. Shortstop has the longest throw to first, considering a batted ball in the hole, the distance between the shortstop and third baseman. Together with the second baseman, double play execution is frequent and important.

The single most important difference: Sure-handed is paramount. Unlike the other infield positions, a slight bobble usually enables the hitter to reach first base safely. The shortstop plays deeper and has a longer throw to first, with little time for recovery. There's also a reason why shortstops can play second or third with ease and why second and third basemen usually find the transition to shortstop very difficult.

2. CATCHER

The roughest position, for sure. I used to marvel at my catcher teammates, wearing all that equipment in hot weather, battered fingers from foul tips, handling pitchers, hitting, when their hands couldn't grip the bat properly, throwing out runners attempting to steal a base, and blocking the plate on runners attempting to score, although the Chase Utley Rule reduced this exercise to a swipe. Say a prayer for catchers. They are a rare breed.

3. SECOND BASE

Executing the double play is the toughest assignment. Pivoting while a runner is bearing down on you takes a lot of skill. Once again, the Chase Utley Rule, while protecting the fielder, results in a lot of wimpiness on double plays. I think fans favor the traditional action over the current trend.

4. THIRD BASE

Swinging bunts are the hardest play for a third baseman. Charging in, fielding the ball, often bare-handed and throwing off-balance to first. Regular bunts are usually anticipated, however, still difficult. Hard hit grounders over the bag, just fair, creates a long throw to first. Quick reflexes are a must. Unlike shortstop, where the ball must be fielded cleanly, a hard hit ball can be blocked with recovery still possible.

5. RIGHT FIELD

Right field requires the strongest arm on the field. With a runner on first base and a ball hit to right field, the right fielder has to prevent the runner from advancing to third. A strong arm is required for this long throw. Also, with lineups usually featuring more right-handed hitters than left, a right-handed hitter's ball will tend to slice away from the fielder toward the foul line. This makes for a difficult adjustment.

6. FIRST BASE

How often have you heard or read, "Oh, stick him on first base."? Usually, this is in reference to a below average fielder. Wrong. It reminds me of a Pete Rose quote on the subject, "People think first base is easy... I've got news for them, it's not." A lot of action takes place around first base: bunts, double plays, scooping up low throws, and so on, all requiring lots of agility.

7. CENTERFIELD

This position requires speed to cover a lot of ground on balls hit to left and right centerfield. A good arm is required, but on balls hit past him, a relay man (infielder) comes out and relays the throw to the appropriate base. Certainly not an easy position, it may be worthy of a higher ranking.

8. LEFT FIELD

My choice for the easiest position is left field. Usually, left fielders have shorter throws, fewer slicing balls, and less ground to cover. It's a good place to figure out your batting average.

CHAPTER FIFTEEN
FANS

I can complain because rose bushes have thorns, or rejoice because thorn bushes have roses. It's all how you look at it.
- J. Kenfield Morley

This chapter is going to be very unusual. Readers, please bear with me. I started writing this chapter for the beginning of the book. I then decided to put it near the end to ensure up-to-date facts for fan information and enjoyment. I decided to leave my original draft intact which really exhibits a sharp contrast between then and now. Shifts in importance have changed dramatically. Here goes.

Original draft: This is a very difficult subject to discuss. It's difficult to draw any conclusions without having a crystal ball handy. Theories abound. There are the doomsayers. These are the people that predict the ruin of baseball every time something out of the ordinary happens, like rule changes, wage increases, slow pace, length of game, and more. Somehow, baseball survives. Analytics is the latest innovation until something else comes along.

The MLB seems to neglect fans. Attendance seems to be less important now than in the past due to huge TV packages, resulting in increased revenues. The players are being rewarded thanks to a strong Players Association Union. Fans are taking a hit with high ticket prices and outlandish concession costs. Parking is another increased expense.

Now the latest hit on small town fans: baseball contraction. Lower Minor League cities affiliated with MLB are being eliminated. MLB wants to slim down to four levels of Minor League baseball. AAA, AA, Advanced A, and Class A. Short season and Rookie Leagues would be eliminated. Chattanooga, Tennessee, is a good example. They have had a Minor League team since 1885. I remember when I played at New Orleans. Harmon Killebrew and Bob Allison eventually had outstanding MLB careers.

Many of these teams and cities facing elimination have invested heavily in stadium improvements, for example. They are family-oriented franchises, in most cases living far from a MLB park. A great example of fan indifference was Nashville, Tennessee, tearing down their stadium near the downtown area in the 1960s. The ballpark was called Sulphur Dell. Built in 1869, it was the most historic park in the country. Nashville was without a team and officially tore the stadium down to make room for a parking lot in 1969. Lack of foresight is an understatement.

The ballpark was unique, with steep hills in the outfield. I talked about it at length in my *Dugouts* book. I'll repeat it here since it was so unusual. Right field was the shortest fence (262 feet) with a 30-foot screen on top of the hill. If you hit a liner over the second baseman's head, you had to run like hell or get thrown out at first by the right fielder. Balls hit off the right-field fence would carom back toward the second baseman. Left and center were deeper, with hills as well. Imagine the difficulty of catching fly balls, while running on a sidehill. Nowadays, they have a new park and team in place. Sulphur Dell should have been preserved. Nothing to do with analytics, just a little sidebar.

Now back to analytics, MLB doesn't seem to care if many fans dislike launching, shifting, exit value, spin rate, and so on. It's here to stay for the time being. As long as teams like Houston (poster team for analytics) keep winning, other teams will try to mimic their organization. Fans yearning for smart ball theories will be ignored. Let's see how long the Astros' success lasts. Their present team is great. They have a very good lineup. Things can change. Right now, they have the personnel to achieve their ultra-analytical style. Time will tell. I favor temperance, as I have attempted to record. Benefits and drawbacks are obvious in most cases. Fans will ultimately decide. Will they stay away in droves? If so, MLB will take notice.

Real Time: The magnitude of baseball's problems is so great that it forced me to alter the title of my book. I started out with

Baseball: Analytics and Beyond and changed it to *Baseball's Future: Analytics and Beyond.*

Well, MLB started their season on July 24th and already there are problems. Three games into the season the Covid-19 virus has caused major problems. The Miami Marlins just completed a three-game series against the Philadelphia Phillies in Philadelphia, PA. Eleven players and two coaches tested positive. They had to remain in Philadelphia and cancel their game in Miami the following night. I hope I'm wrong, but I predicted that the season wouldn't start or last long if it did. The short sixty-game season is in jeopardy. I can't imagine thirty teams competing effectively with expected depleted rosters. Time will tell.

Many of the things I mentioned in my original draft have been forced to be put on hold, pending 2021 MLB circumstances. Foremost is the Houston Astros' cheating scandal in 2017 and 2018. Houston received a pass, due to the all-consuming virus concern.

Spring training incidents proved that all was not forgotten. Some opponent players reportedly mocked them and engaged in verbal abuse. Just this morning, a report stated that Los Angeles Dodgers' pitcher Joe Kelly was suspended for eight games for throwing at several Houston hitters. Hard feelings remain, as LA feels that Houston "stole" the World Series title from them in 2017 with their sign-stealing scandal. LA feels that eight games was a harsh penalty, considering the short sixty-game season.

So it remains to be seen how fans will react to baseball and all sports for that matter for the rest of 2020 and beyond. My final chapter, Conclusions, should provide some insight for fans to reflect on for the coming hopefully normal 2021 season.

Sulphur Dell – Nashville – 1961

CHAPTER SIXTEEN
Respect

> Most of all, differences of opinion are opportunities for learning.
>
> - Terry Tempest Williams

The late American comedian Rodney Dangerfield was known for his self-deprecating humor. We remember his using the catchphrase: "I get no respect." Throughout my research on analytics, for the purpose of fair representation of both affirmative and negative viewpoints on this subject, I'm reminded of analytic-favored bias. It reminds me of politics. Various authors and analytical advocates often insult people with opposing viewpoints. I want to ask these advocates, "Can we get along?" This, of course, doesn't share the importance of this famous quote from the late African American Los Angeles, California, resident, Rodney King. The taped video led to the 1992 LA riots.

So on a much lighter scale, can we get along with our different opinions? I think of all the great players I played with and against – nineteen Hall of Fame members if Pete Rose ever gets inducted. Players like Mickey Mantle, Billy Williams, Ron Santo, Phil Niekro, Bob Gibson, Denny McClain, Brooks Robinson, and Carl Yastrzemski, to name a few. More recent players like Mike Schmidt, Steve Carlton, Derek Jeter, Mariano Rivera, and countless others come to mind. When I hear remarks praising current players and diminishing accomplishments of past eras, I get angry.

With baseball on hold due to the Covid-19 virus pandemic, I sense an attitude change in some players. I think fans were beginning to lose some respect for high salaried, low hustle players. Many players donated their money and services to areas in need during this crisis. Perhaps they are putting things into perspective, realizing it's only a game. Surely, fans would welcome this change, and players would regain their lost respect.

Well, it's late September with only a few remaining games left in this shortened season. Chapter 17: Interviews should be finished before the World Series. Looks like a possible Yankees vs. Dodgers World Series. Eight teams from each league will make the playoffs. I'll repeat an earlier statement that I love baseball, but I can't really get enthused about watching this mediocre, tainted season. It will provide or at least raise a lot of questions on the title of this book, *Baseball's Future: Analytics and Beyond!* There will be more on this in Chapter 18, along with my final observations.

Bill, Ellen, Pete Rose

CHAPTER SEVENTEEN

Interviews

This chapter has lived up to the expectations I perceived when I first decided to write another book. With such a controversial subject as baseball analytics, I thought that fans' opinions would lend a bipartisan touch to the overall book content. I was right. My objective at the outset was to keep politics out of my research. Both sides must be heard. Benefits and drawbacks of baseball analytics and its invasion of baseball was my goal. My interviews ranged from baseball fans with limited knowledge of analytics to fans familiar with analytics, and even some with high school and college coaching positions.

Before I begin the actual interviews, I must share the most memorable comment on analytics upon asking Neal Kline, a member of our weekly golf group, about his thoughts on analytics in baseball. His reply: What the f... is analytics?" A classic comment.

As I stated in the prologue, my goal in writing this book was to make the theories currently permeating today's baseball scene more understandable to the average baseball fan. This was so important to me that I decided to devote a chapter to interviews. I include opinions from my friends and even strangers I met during book signings and other meetings.

One of my initial persons to interview was Sam Tropiano who had just finished his thirty-first season as head baseball coach of the prestigious Bishop Eustace Preparatory School, located in Pennsauken NJ. Sam, a Villanova University graduate (bachelor's & master's degrees), has compiled a career win-loss record of 686-251. His teams at Eustace have made the state tournament every year. My thoughts of providing a younger generation flavor to the analytic topic were realized.

While Sam believes in the value of some analytic theories, he also subscribes to the temperance of those ideas. He pointed out the small sample of data for computer use, due to the fact that teams usually face each other only twice, sometimes less often, during the season. Prior to the interview, Sam introduced me to a computer-savvy undergraduate who works with the team, collecting data and so forth. Obviously, Sam wouldn't have compiled his outstanding record without teaching all of the basic fundamentals. From my playing experience, these are basically physical instructions. I was impressed with Sam's mental (analytics) teaching: teamwork, teammate respect, in-game concentration, and so on. Sam said, "I never want to look over at our dugout and see someone's back." He stresses team unity. Everyone truly pulls for each other. "When everyone exhibits this trait, a winning attitude is established." Individually, I was impressed with Sam's video practice. During each game, a player's plate appearances are recorded and given to each player for his home computer analysis. Great idea!

I was also impressed with Sam's coaching philosophies. Sam is well versed in the analytical era teachings; however, he also incorporates some traditional methods. On hitting, he adheres basically to three steps: (1) mechanics – less movement, (2) approach – zone hitting (one side of the plate), situation hitting (different pitch counts 2-0, 0-2, 3-1, etc., and (3) mental – focus and toughness.

Sam believes launching, a popular analytic term, is misinterpreted. Traditional teaching of hitting down on the ball (actually level), resulting in meeting the ball at the equator, is preferred over an uppercut swing. Home runs will still be achieved.

I agree with Sam's dislike of specialization in youth sports today. Sam says, "Baseball is the worst sport for specialization" with the resulting overuse of the arm in pitching and lack of quality conditioning for position players. I always thought playing basketball really helped me in my baseball career.

Sam also pointed out the difficulty of baseball, with a failure rate of seven out of ten batting attempts. You succeed three out of ten times if you're a .300 hitter. Equate that rate to business, and you're fired.

My second interview with Sam was very timely. He had just returned from Nashville, Tennessee, after attending the ABCA (American Baseball Coaches Association) convention. The four-day convention featured 7,100 coaches and over 350 companies that manufacture baseball products and more than 50 clinics. Sam said analytics was obviously dominant and "not going away anytime soon."

Special thanks to Sam for taking the time from his very busy schedule for the interviews. Also for the analytical pamphlets he provided which proved to be valuable research assets. Thank you, Sam, a Hall of Fame coach, for sure.

Bill Wagner is a long-time friend two years behind me at Woodrow Wilson High School in Camden, New Jersey. When I first got the idea to have a chapter on interviews in my book, I thought of two individuals, Sam Tropiano at the high school level and Bill Wagner at the college level for usage in their respective careers.

Bill was an outstanding three-sport star in baseball, football, and basketball in high school and college (Trenton State College, New Jersey). In fact, he earned Player of the Year in all three sports his senior year. Fantastic accomplishment. Bill played semi-pro baseball for six decades.

Bill coached high school – three sports for nine years. Several titles. He coached baseball at University of Pennsylvania, assistant coach, pitching coach – 34 years / 634 wins /five Ivy League titles / 5 trips to Regional NCAA / 1970 – 2005 – Lowest ERA 1988 NCAA. Several players were drafted, and a few like Mark DeRosa, Steve Atkins, and Doug Glanville made it to the Major Leagues. Bill also coached football at Penn for 50 years, 1970 to 2020, just recently retiring. This produced five championships, two undefeated seasons, and over 1,500 athletes that Bill coached and saw graduate from Penn.

Bill has received many individual honors and awards as a player and coach. South Jersey Baseball Hall of Fame, Maxwell Lifetime Achievement Award, Philadelphia Sports Writer Award, College Player of The Year Award (Trenton State College), and several high school and college awards as a player and coach.

Is it any wonder that I sought out my friend for his well-qualified thoughts on baseball analytics? As a player and coach, his observations reflect much of my research on the subject. His comments show the progression of analytics in the early days, (not called analytics then) to the present. Bill argues that analytics was present years ago, via word of mouth and knowing the tendencies of players and teams. Coaches and players always made adjustments to both, wanting to take advantage of various situations – hitting, pitching, and offensive and defensive strategy.

Bill correctly states that in earlier years, football used technology to break down situations and tendencies for all facets of the game. Meanwhile, baseball did it by hand with charting pitches and players, as well as using stats to your advantage. He feels that in the last ten years, with technology advances, all sports have increased their analytical approach to the players' performances and to coaches' planning and teaching techniques that have changed the game. Uppercut swings of batters trying to launch homeruns are producing more homeruns and more strikeouts. Pitchers trying to counter the uppercut swing are working higher in the strike zone. Result: fewer fly balls, but when they miss, the result is more homeruns. Defensively, the infield shift has taken away so many hits because of the style of swing and less bat control, creating holes in the batters swing.

Bill predicts that overshifting, launching, and so on will go full cycle, a return to hitting through the ball, driving into the gap, and ground balls. This, rather than pop-ups, strikeouts, and 12-10 scores with four or five pitchers every game and not many complete games by pitchers. He feels that all of this will result in getting back to the fundamentals of the game.

Bill has certainly given my readers many interesting aspects of analytics to ponder. Many of his expressions are covered in more detail throughout the book. Thank you, Bill, for your insights.

It's not Just About the Analytics

My dentist, Saul N. Miller, DDS, came through again. When I asked him if he would like to opine on analytics in baseball, he offered some very insightful opinions. Not slighting any of my other interviewees, Dr. Miller really went beyond analytics, touching on skill development, teammates, and various psychological theories. With his gracious permission, I have decided to write it in its entirety.

The numbers don't lie, but they don't necessarily tell the whole story. Players or anyone can have the best numbers, statistics, grades, or whatever, but can they put all the skills together seamlessly to excel consistently? Does the player with great stats inspire his teammates to be better, or is the star on stat-overload a cancer that ultimately sinks the team ship? Does the analytics staff have any understanding of people and the game, and can the algorithm put a team together that is a cohesive one whose stats and personalities mesh for a winning formula? Of course, the manager and coaching staff must also have the ability and style to keep everyone going in the same direction.

A team based on the analytics of its individual players can also be a boring team and an unsuccessful team. When players have been taught to succeed based primarily on the analytical assessment of their individual skills, they may never truly reach the level of expert. According to the Dreyfus Model of skill development, an expert solves problems or situations that often arrive with the speed of a fastball or the path of a curveball. On one end of the scale, the novice analyzes the problem, consciously plugs in a recipe to solve it but takes no responsibility for the outcome, feeling that outside factors are the reason for failure. The expert, however, recognizes the problem, knows what is important and what is not, and intuitively knows what to do to achieve the expected result, along with taking ownership of the outcome. In fact, the expert may not be able to explain the solution to the non-expert because each stage of learning, from novice through expert, is now part of the overall thought process and emotional involvement.

Like so many other skills in and out of baseball, hitting can be considered an art as well as a science. It takes love of the game and its parts along with the ability to persevere over time to achieve excellence, and then it takes continual work to maintain that excellence, especially when the inevitable slump or "yips" show up. In other words, it takes grit, and the grit must not end after the big payday. Studies have shown that when education and experience are equal, grit, defined by Angela Duckworth as "passionate pursuit of long term goals" is often the determining factor in the level of success achieved. The struggle is real.

Dr. Duckworth, a University of Pennsylvania psychology professor, also wrote, "Talent + Consistent Effort = Skill and Skill + Consistent Effort = Achievement." So numbers do not lie, but by omission, they may not tell the whole truth. In part, analytics and numbers are important in baseball, but baseball may be considered a metaphor for life with all the complexities that are encountered and the need for team players, who are experts, to work together to solve them.

Ron Rossi Jr., son of my good friend Ron Rossi, whom I mentioned in several chapters, is an amazing athlete. Ron is still playing baseball, in his fifties. Although his best sport was football, he has an impressive resume of semi-pro baseball participation. Ron's list: the Pittsburgh (PA) Federation League, Rancocas Valley League (NJ), Atlantic County League (NJ), and the prestigious Bridgeton Invitational Tournament (NJ) for twenty years. Ron has also coached baseball at the high school and junior college level. Remarkable, considering baseball is his second best sport, having had an outstanding career in football at the University of Delaware. Ron's position: defensive end and is eighth on the all-time sack list. Good job, Ron.

Ron had some interesting comments on analytics in baseball. He echoes some of my points in chapter ten on Shifting. He mentions Ryan Howard and Scott Kingery of the Philadelphia Phillies changing their swing to achieve a launch angle advocated by analytic experts. I agree with Ron on line drives and hard grounders being valuable.

Ron says that's how he was taught. Homeruns would come with hard contact.

Ron says, "Outlaw the shift to save the game." More strikeouts and fewer balls in play make a boring game. All good thoughts and opinions.

My publisher Tim Renfrow has some very strong opinions on analytics in baseball. "They ruin the game." Tim says in early times analytics were used but under a different name – small ball. Strategizing on scoring a single run to win a game, as opposed to today's search for home runs on every swing, is no longer part of the game. "Analytics suck the heart out of the game in every way." Tim says, "There is nothing like seeing a below average hitter smacking the ball out of the ballpark when the game is on the line." "Or seeing a pitcher will his way through a final inning even though the skipper knows that it is dangerous to do so." He says today that would never happen. Like many people, he can barely watch today's games and cares for it less as time goes by. I asked and Tim surely responded.

I can always count on my son Ben Davidson to provide some insightful comments in our sports conversations. Ben feels that baseball analytics so prevalent in today's games could very well swing back to the middle in time. A case in point is the heavy emphasis on fly balls and home runs; hitters changing their swings to accommodate a slight uppercut for the long ball as opposed to line drives and hard grounders. Ben likens it to all golfers not having the same swing. He also would like to see statistics on errors – fly balls vs. grounders. Very interesting, since errors provide base runners, potential runs, and wins. Analytical proponents will not easily concede their philosophies.

Not to be outdone, my other son Will, known as the "first born," as he has been known to say, provided some interesting comments on analytics in baseball. Will says baseball analytics is a great tool. He thinks statistical baseball models often miss the finer details that only human experience can define. It's tricky, don't be fooled by the numbers. He likes the North Carolina state motto – "Esse Quam Videri" which means "To be, rather than to seem."

My sister Kathy Davidson is a big baseball fan (Phillies). Kathy played softball and coached the Pennsauken High School girls softball team. Like most of the people I have interviewed, she acknowledges the current analytical craze but decries the dismissal of small ball. Kathy prefers the old traditional brand of baseball. She was happy to see Gabe Kapler, the Philadelphia Phillies manager, replaced.

Let's take a timeout on interviews and get up to date on the MLB playoff happenings. It's mid-October, and my prediction of a Yankee vs. Dodgers World Series won't materialize. The Tampa Bay Rays eliminated the Yankees, and the Dodgers are down 2-0 vs. the Atlanta Braves. Tampa is up 3-0 vs. Houston. I still can't get enthused in this pandemic, 60-game, fanless season. I have yet to watch a game. Back to the interviews.

My brother-in-law, Jim Ackley, is a big sports enthusiast and expressed his displeasure with baseball analytics. We have some good baseball conversations, and Jim usually has some astute observations. Jim laments the passing of baseball and the way it was played in the not-to-distant past. He feels the players played with their "heart," as opposed to today's players with their multi-million dollar contracts. Jim hates analytically minded managers' handling of starter and relief pitchers, with starters rarely going more than 5 innings and a parade of 1-inning relief pitchers. Jim cites the late Robin Roberts of the Philadelphia Phillies as an example. Robin's record of pitching all 17 innings in an extra-inning game on September 6, 1952, is a remarkable contrast to today's game. Robin's line: 17 innings, 16 hits, 6 runs, and 3 walks. Today's pitchers ice their shoulders and elbows after pitching a game. Robin said he "took a hot shower and ran hot water on my arm."

My close friend Rocky Iacovone, a good semi-pro baseball player, offered his opinion on analytics in baseball. We had a spirited conversation on the pros and cons of analytics. We were generally on the same page in favoring the old school smart ball techniques. Rocky was in favor of the shifting philosophies now in vogue. My feelings were somewhat different, as expressed in Chapter 10. I enjoyed our friendly conversation.

Mihir Patel is a big baseball fan, and he has expressed displeasure with analytics in today's game. Mihir is the owner of the local liquor store and agreed to opine for my interview chapter. He dislikes analytics in general and thinks that the heart of the game is missing. He doesn't favor the all-or-nothing approach. His feelings echo many of the interviews I have conducted.

Mike Toryk, produce manager at the local BJ's wholesale grocery store in Maple Shade, New Jersey, thought that analytics has its place (more data). But he felt that managers were leaning too much on analytics and less on feel of the game when making decisions.

Thank you to all who took the time to respond to my interview requests for this chapter. The interviews proved to be very thought provoking and should encourage readers to form their own judgments on the pros and cons of analytics in baseball.

CHAPTER EIGHTEEN

Conclusions

It's official. The LA Dodgers are World Champions. Congratulations! I'm sure my friend Ron Rossi is happy. Even though it was a 60-game season, they deserved it. They probably would have won it in a regular 162-game season. They overcame a 3-1 deficit to beat the Atlanta Braves in the National League Championship Series and took care of Tampa Bay 4-2 in the World Series. Tampa Bay beat Houston in the American League Championship Series.

Game six of the series stirred up some controversy. Analytics came under close scrutiny and was responsible in some quarters for the loss. Ron and Dodger fans alike were probably ecstatic when Tampa Manager Kevin Cash took starting left-handed pitcher Blake Snell out of the game in the sixth inning after holding the Dodgers to two hits and no runs. Post-game remarks were abundant. Manager Cash said he didn't want Snell to face the Dodgers upcoming trio of Mookie Betts, Corey Seager, and Justin Turner for a third time. Analytics? Was it an analytical-minded manager favoring a popular analytical theory: limiting starter innings in favor of a relief pitcher? Who knows? It seems to be a classic example of analytical micromanagement. This sounds ludicrous to me, however, the controversy remains. Mookie commented that he and other players were happy, as they were having difficulty with Snell who had retired 16 batters and allowed 2 singles. His pitch count was only 73 and he had 9 strikeouts. Second guessing and Monday morning quarterbacking aside, this was not a shining moment for analytical proponents. Snell deserved to remain in the game for at least another hitter or two.

I have to admit, I lost some interest with this Covid-19 season and watched very few games. I was glad the Houston Astros lost, since they had received a pass on opposition retaliation for their cheating scandal the past few years. This team has a lot of talent but needs to shed their "hot dog" tendencies. No class.

To put things in perspective, I started my book in October 2019, well before the Covid-19 pandemic struck. My research on analytics in baseball began with some interviews. Although my research continued, the MLB 2020 season obviously became less important. Health issues were a major concern. Therefore, the short 2020 season was not an accurate barometer for analytical progress or regression in baseball. Hopefully, 2021 will bring a normal season and a more educated prognosis for the direction of analytics and baseball in general. Nevertheless, life went on, and I proceeded with my book-writing objectives.

MLB, like all major professional sports, took a hard hit from the pandemic. The short season resulted in large revenue losses. Television money was the only source of revenue. Attendance, parking, and concession stand money were no longer at its disposal. Even though the owners are multi-millionaires, they had to make financial decisions for both the 2020 season and the uncertain 2021 season. Teams are unsure of the wisdom of investing in multi-year contracts to star players and hesitate to sign players who are scheduled to become free agents. They risk losing these players. Even front office personnel face dismissal.

I live in the Philadelphia area (Cherry Hill, NJ) and notice that the Philadelphia Phillies have a dilemma with their star catcher, J.T. Realmuto. His hitting and fielding make him arguably the best all-around catcher in MLB. He is a free agent and only thirty years old. He is very durable but catching is brutal. and five years from now at thirty-five, will the position have taken its toll on his body, particularly his knees? Therefore, teams must weigh long-term contracts with astronomical figures vs. future durability. Of course fans and owners have opposing viewpoints.

Even before Covid-19, MLB faced big problems. Attendance figures were down. Fans cited long games and analytics when questioned. The interviews I conducted revealed an overwhelmingly negative consensus on analytics and baseball's future.

I have some interesting observations on analytics brought on by the short season and hurried playoff schedule. Things were happening that made analytics-inclined managers switch their tactics to more traditional strategies. They were bunting more, even stealing a base on occasion. Due to the extreme shifts, I've never seen so many infield hits. Using a minor league rule – place a man on second base in extra inning games – reawakened some managers to the art of bunting. Some players forgot how to bunt. What happened to the home run swing? Could smart ball be making a comeback? Probably not, we'll just have to wait for 2021 to find out. Excuse me for being so cynical, but, as I said previously, more teams might have made the playoffs, instead of sitting at home watching if they had played this way the entire season. The short season exposed the questionable wisdom of extreme analytical thinking in baseball.

So it's mid-November 2020 and only three months or so until spring training 2021. It's difficult to predict MLB's immediate future. Will Covid-19 allow a full 2021 schedule? Will fan displeasure with analytics in general and extreme analytically-minded managers prevail? Will a looming strike occur? Baseball has managed to survive many problems over the years. 2021 could perhaps be the ultimate test.

An update on MLB and its Minor League contraction plans, which I wrote about in Chapter 9: Player Development. My worse fears were realized. As I mention throughout the book, it's all about money. Money and control. MLB threw many small-town baseball franchises under the bus. Some of these towns will either have no baseball or an inferior version than what they had known. As I explained previously, Minor League franchises have been affiliated with MLB teams which supply players and monetary assistance. But things change. MLB has either eliminated franchises or downgraded them. AAA, AA, and high A will survive. Below these, low A and some short-season leagues will disappear. Some will become Independent League members, which hasn't the same prestigious quality as being affiliated with an MLB team. Now all thirty MLB teams will have to follow an MLB allotment which will be equal. Final details are still being worked out. As you know, nothing ever remains the same. Stay tuned, fans.

Just when I thought I had finished my Conclusions chapter, I read an article today that presented some observations for a few closing comments on analytics. Once again, "poster child on analytics in baseball," Trevor Bauer, comes to the forefront. It's really fitting that Bauer dominated much of my research in the beginning of the book, then he reappears at the close. Anyway, the Philadelphia Phillies just hired a new pitching coach, Caleb Cotham. Caleb is only thirty-three and made his MLB debut in 2015 with the New York Yankees, managed by Joe Girardi, the current Phillies manager. Due to injuries, Caleb's career ended by 2016.

The article grabbed my attention when his background revealed some of my research sources on analytics. Like Trevor Bauer, Driveline Baseball and their cutting-edge technologies had shaped Caleb's pitching philosophies, all of which I mentioned in earlier chapters. The Bauer connection: Caleb was assistant pitching coach for the Cincinnati Reds. Cy Young Award winner Bauer had someone to talk to and with whom to share ideas. Caleb and Girardi seem to be on the same page. Both appreciate a science-based approach as well as traditional methods. I respect Girardi's judgment and feel that this chapter can end with the hope of a successful marriage of the two theories.

DEFINITIONS

BABI P – Batting Average Balls In Play.
Measures how many of a Batter's balls in play go for hits, or how many balls in play against a pitcher go for hits, excluding homeruns

BB9/W_IP – Walks per nine innings pitched.

BF or TBF – Batters faced or total bvatters faced.

DRA – Deserved Run Average

DRS – Defensive Runs Saved

DIPS – Defense Independent Pitching Statistics
Stats that do not involve fielders, except catcher.

Exit Velocity – Speed in which ball comes off bat.

FIP – Fielding Independent Pitching

Five Tool Player – Speed, Throwing, Fielding, Hitting for average, Hitting for power. (Physical Tools)

FRAA – Fielding Runs Above Average

Launching Angle – The vertical angle at which the ball leaves a player's bat after being struck.
Avg. Launch Angle - 2015 – 10.5 2016 – 11.5 2017 – 12.0 degrees

OBP – On base percentage. Hits, walks, hit by pitch.

OPS – On base plus slugging.

SABERMETRICS – The empirical analysis of baseball, especially baseball stats that measure in-game activity.
Coined by Bill James.

SO9/SO_IP – Strikeouts per nine innings pitched

SO/BB – Ratio of strikeouts to walks

STATCAST – Tracking technology used by MLB to gather data on everything from pitcher velocity, spin rate and release to hitters' exit velocity and launch angle..

UZR – Ultimate Zone Rating. A defensive metric that uses zone data to determine how good a fielder a particular player is. They use a player's range instead of simply the balls he has an opportunity to field. Thought to be more reliable than traditional stats like errors and fielding percentage.

WHIP – Walks plus hits per innings pitched.

WAR – Wins Above Replacement
Measures "value" of a player to his team vs. an often described inferior "replacement player."

INDEX

Made in the USA
Middletown, DE
19 March 2021

35342439R00080